LONG ISLAND
MIGRANT
LABOR CAMPS

Dear Mary Anne,
Thanks for your
support!

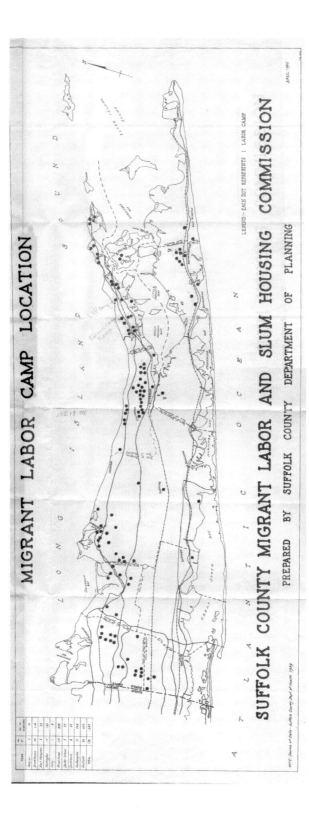

MIGRANT LABOR CAMP LOCATION

LEGEND:- EACH DOT REPRESENTS 1 LABOR CAMP

SUFFOLK COUNTY MIGRANT LABOR AND SLUM HOUSING COMMISSION

PREPARED BY SUFFOLK COUNTY DEPARTMENT OF PLANNING

APRIL 1960

LONG ISLAND
MIGRANT
LABOR CAMPS

DUST FOR BLOOD

MARK A. TORRES

THE
History
PRESS

Published by The History Press
Charleston, SC
www.historypress.com

Frontispiece: Migrant Labor Camp Location map created in 1960 by the Suffolk County Migrant Labor and Slum Housing Commission. Each dotted mark denotes the location of a labor camp in the county. At the time that this map was created, there were 120 labor camps in Suffolk County that housed nearly two thousand migrant farmworkers. *Courtesy of the Southold Historical Society, Southold Historical Society, Southold, New York.*

First published 2021

Manufactured in the United States

ISBN 9781467147842

Library of Congress Control Number: 2020948628

For my wife and children, who complete me.

CONTENTS

CONTENTS

AUTHOR'S NOTE

This book chronicles the history of the migrant labor camps in Suffolk County, New York, during the twentieth century. To those who do not reside on the eastern end of Long Island, the very notion that slum-like labor camps existed less than one hundred miles from New York City must seem like nothing more than rural folklore. Even those who might have known of their existence are likely unaware of the full extent of their history. But they did exist, and it is the obscurity of this history that inspired me to chronicle this story so that it can be known and studied and, most importantly, remembered.

Suffolk County is an area known for its rich history. However, information on the migrant labor camps is surprisingly scant. After an exhaustive search, no comprehensive primary or even secondary source chronicling this region's dark topic could be located. Most of the individuals who were directly affected are deceased. Details of the camps are rare and, in most cases, other than a general street name in a specific town or hamlet, they remain a mystery. Thus in far too many ways, much of this history is truly lost, and gathering information about this topic more than half a century from the camps' heyday, proved to be dramatically challenging. Undeterred, I continued my research, and the deeper I delved into this history, the greater my obligation grew to tell it.

History can be a stubborn thing. Lingering personal accounts of life, exploitation and death have been shared by a handful of individuals who bore witness to this era, along with a few documentarians and local news reporters, all of whom strived to inform the public about the migrant labor camps that once dominated the region. Now, nearly eighty years after the first camp was established, this book shines a bright light on a story that has been long buried and very nearly forgotten. It raises, in the conscious mind, the camp structures that have long since vanished. Most importantly, it lends a voice to the thousands of migrants who came to Long Island each year in search of work, housing and dignity only to find abuse, misery and, in some cases, death. For if we lack the resolve to report the full history, then that history truly disappears, leaving an irreplaceable void.

The information in this book was gathered from hundreds of news articles written by respectable reporters of the time. A few short documentary films were particularly instrumental and quite illuminating. Several tangentially related literary pieces, along with some good old-fashioned investigative work, which included numerous interviews with people familiar with the subject, were also critical to my research.

On my journey, I visited with local clergy at various places of worship. I also met with incredibly bright and sincere local historians and librarians whose diligence and passion are always appreciated. I contacted local activist groups for assistance, many of whom were borne from a cause like the one featured in this story. I also spoke with several farmers from the area to gain their valuable perspective. A wide-sweeping information request filed with the Suffolk County Department of Health and other government agencies yielded over one thousand documents. Clearly, very few stones were left unturned, as the importance of this topic demanded it.

Despite the dark subject matter, I also learned about special individuals who, both in their personal and professional capacities, were very active in the fight to improve the conditions faced by migrant workers on Long Island. I had the good fortune to meet and befriend family members of these individuals who passionately shared stories and information about their long-lost loved ones. Our conversations were both informative and inspirational, and I felt obligated to properly capture their legacies in this book.

Lastly, although this book focuses on local history that is limited to a specific region and time period, it is but a microcosm of the plight faced by farmworkers throughout the nation for many years. More importantly, their plight continues today, and there is still a great amount of work needed to achieve justice for farmworkers in the United States and beyond. Local and national advocacy groups strive to extend federal and state labor law protection for farmworkers and to promote higher wages, better working conditions, access to health care and job safety information and immigration reform, all of which can help end the rampant discrimination and exploitation of those who work so hard to help feed our nation. For more information on how you can help, I encourage you to connect with local or national groups who tirelessly advocate for farmworkers each and every day. Every little bit does indeed help.

A man, a community, a civilization either takes responsibility or it does not. There is no middle course. To have seen with one's own eyes the terrible price of indifference, be it global or local, is lesson enough. Or is it?

—Got to Move

ACKNOWLEDGEMENTS

This book is dedicated to my wife, Migdalia Ortiz-Torres, whose spirit, strength, love and belief in me, along with her much-needed critical thinking, careful analysis and diligent research, have made this book possible.

This book is also dedicated to my children, Isabella, Jake and Olivia, who continue to inspire me every day to be a better father, person, teacher and writer. I would also like to thank my mother, Grace, whose strength knows no bounds, along with my family, friends and colleagues for their dedicated and unending support.

This book is also dedicated to all the warriors who persist in the labor movement and who collectively understand that an injustice anywhere in the workplace is an injustice everywhere in the workplace. I also dedicate this book to the memory of all the farmworkers and families referenced in this story and to all those who presently toil each and every day to help feed the greatest nation on earth. They deserve so much more and have been neglected for far too long.

I have a great deal of respect and appreciation to the many individuals whose enthusiastic support made the completion of this book possible. They include, but by no means are limited to, Melissa Andruski, Caroline Axelrod Wendy Polhemus-Annibell, Harvey Aronson, Janice Artandi, Eileen Bryant, Maureen Bryant, Ismael Garcia-Colon, Joseph Daugherty, Carlos DeJesus, Grace Dotson, Amy Folk, Joseph Grattan, Maggie Gray, Karl Grossman, Louisa Hargrave, Maria Hinojosa, Laurence I. Hewes III, Paul Jeffers Jr., Lee Koppelman, Leslie Mashmann, Veronica Martinez-Matsuda, Daniel

Acknowledgements

McCarthy, Pamela McCartney, Doug Morris, Raymond Nelson, Jerie Newman, Kathleen Goggin Nickels, Mariella Ostraski, Daniel Perl, William Prince, Pierce Rafferty, William Sanok, Monica Schnee, Susan Van Scoy, Martin Sidor, Chris Verga, Jeff Walden, Donna Watkins, Jim Wall, Jeff Walden, Steve Wick, Tom Wickham, Janice Young and Joseph Zuhoski.

The following organizations, and the wonderful people associated with them, provided tremendous support for my research: Center for Puerto Rican Studies at Hunter College, Cutchogue New Suffolk Free Library, Eastern Farmworkers Association, East Hampton Public Library, Floral Park Public Library, Floyd Memorial Library (Greenport), Glen Cove Public Library, Hallocksville Museum Farm, Henry L. Ferguson Museum (Fishers Island), Mattituck Laurel Library, Ohio State University Mahn Center for Archives and Special Collections, Oysterponds Historical Society, Shelter Island Historical Society, Shelter Island Public Library, Southold Historical Society, Stirling Historical Society, Stony Brook University, Suffolk County Department of Health, Suffolk County Historical Society and the Water Mill Museum. I would also like to thank J. Banks Smither and the amazing team at The History Press/Arcadia Publishing for their assistance in making this book possible.

INTRODUCTION

During the early morning hours of October 8, 1961, the tranquil North Fork of Long Island, New York, was suddenly disturbed by the blaring alarms of fire trucks careening through the countryside. Their destination was a raging fire at the infamous farm labor camp on Cox Lane in Cutchogue. For years, the camp had been used to house hundreds of migrant farmworkers who traveled from other states to harvest potatoes and other crops on the vast farms of Long Island.

The fire began after a leaky kerosene stove exploded inside one of the camp's barracks.[1] Within minutes, flames engulfed the one-hundred-by-twenty-five-foot wooden structure. It took several hours and over 120 firefighters to extinguish the blaze. When they did, they learned that the fire had claimed the lives of Leroy McKoy, James Davis and Charles Jordan. A fourth man, identified as James Overstreet, died later that day from his injuries at a nearby hospital. The other occupants of the barracks barely escaped without injury.

Local police investigated the scene and discovered that one of the men attempted to light the kerosene stove, and excess oil, which had leaked nearby, caused the explosion. Detectives further learned that, although kerosene stoves were barred, the stove that caused the fire was snuck in by the migrant workers to use for cooking because they struggled to afford the seventy-five-cent cost for meals at the camp. Despite the four deaths, the fire was ultimately ruled to be an accident, and no charges were filed.

The deadly incident at the Cutchogue camp was by no means exclusive. There were other catastrophic fires at several labor camps or makeshift structures inhabited by migrant farmworkers. In November 1950, two children in Bridgehampton perished when the twelve-by-twenty-foot chicken coop they had been inhabiting with their family erupted into flames.[2] In an eleven-day span in early 1959, various fires claimed the lives of eight people, including Nathanial Cobb, who burned to death in a rundown shack at the Hollis Warner duck farm in Riverhead.[3] Just one week earlier, a woman named Dilsia Trent was forced to abandon her three young children, who died in a raging fire at a shanty in Riverhead. The young mother suffered burns on over 80 percent of her body before succumbing to her injuries.[4] A few days later, separate fires claimed the lives of two small children, who died from asphyxiation, and a man who burned to death in a dilapidated shack. Later that year, a total of three more lives were claimed by fire, including Herman Howard, who died when a two-burner kerosene stove he was using exploded, causing a fire to immediately engulf the one-room shanty he inhabited.[5]

Over the years, random fires claimed more lives. In 1963, fifteen-month-old Joseph W. Jones and his three-month-old sister, Elizabeth, burned to death when a fire swept through their twenty-by-twenty-foot shack at the Hollis Warner duck farm in Riverhead.[6] On January 14, 1968, Myrtle Lee Grant, along with James Farrell and Gussie Farrell, burned to death at the Jacobs labor camp in Bridgehampton. In that fire, investigators found that the door to their sleeping quarters was reportedly nailed shut to keep out the frigid draft.[7]

The ages of the victims and the locations of these tragedies all vary, but the grim results were all very much the same, their commonalities unmistakable. All of the victims were impoverished migrant laborers who lived in cramped, slum-like quarters that were not fit for human habitation, and the use of portable kerosene stoves or heaters were the unwitting instruments of death.

Along with the inherent physical dangers of inhabiting labor camps, the thousands of migrant workers who were lured to Long Island each year with promises of good wages and decent housing instead found themselves mired in irrevocable debt and despair, burdened by physical and mental hardships and left powerless to effect any change in their conditions. One local advocate described the Suffolk County migratory labor camp system as a "20th Century form of slavery."[8] All of this took place in one of the most scenic and affluent counties in the United States and less than one hundred miles from New York City. What would subject people to live, and die, in such conditions? The answer to this question can only be uncovered by a careful review of the conditions at these labor camps, who operated them and why.

Long Island Migrant Labor Camps: Dust for Blood is the riveting, comprehensive and never before told true story about the migrant labor camps in Suffolk County from their inception during World War II, through their heyday in 1960 and culminating with their steady decline by the end of the twentieth century. This book will chronicle the many aspects of this dark history, including the human suffering of the camps' inhabitants, the cause and effect of these camps and the factors that led to their eventual decline. This book will also feature the heroic efforts of special individuals who, in their own unique ways, were outspoken critics of the deplorable conditions of these camps and fought to improve the lot of migrant workers on the eastern end of Long Island.

1

LONG ISLAND

Fertile Land

Long Island is an island on the Atlantic Ocean that comprises the southeasternmost part of New York State.[9] It is divided into two counties: Nassau County lies in the western portion and Suffolk County is to the east. According to the U.S. Census Bureau, Suffolk is the second largest and easternmost county in New York. It occupies 66 percent of the land area of Long Island and has an area of 2,373 square miles with 980 miles of coastline. This book focuses exclusively within the geographical boundaries of Suffolk County.

Approximately seventy-five miles east of New York City is the first of two peninsulas on the eastern end of Long Island, known as the North Fork. Adjacent to a large tidal estuary called the Long Island Sound, the North Fork is approximately thirty miles long. The other peninsula, known as the South Fork, runs parallel to its counterpart to the north, albeit slightly longer, and abuts the Atlantic Ocean, extending all the way to Montauk. The forks split at the town of Riverhead, and in between them is the Peconic River, which has its own set of small islands, including Gardiner's Island, Robins Island and Shelter Island. The eastern part of the county includes Riverhead, Southampton, Southold, Shelter Island and East Hampton. The towns in the western part of the county are Babylon, Brookhaven, Huntington, Islip and Smithtown. This entire area was created thousands of years ago when expanding glaciers ground against the landmass, leaving a terrain with extremely rich topsoil. From the Native American inhabitants all the way up to owners of the modern-day vineyards, this fertile land has always yielded an abundance of crops to all who have settled in this area.

Much of Suffolk County has always been known for large agricultural production. Founded by Puritans in 1640, the town of Southold and its surrounding hamlets have long been the home of families like the Tuthills and Wickhams, who have been farming in this area for generations. Throughout the nineteenth century, the population of New York grew so rapidly that it doubled each decade. Immigrants from Ireland, Germany, Poland and other parts of eastern Europe arrived, and many began to settle in Suffolk County.[10] These settlers brought their skill in potato harvesting to the farms of Long Island. The potato was highly favored because it is a major source of vitamins, minerals and dietary fiber and offers a great amount of energy with little fat content. The fertile land of Suffolk County coupled with the knowledge of growing potatoes led to a sharp increase in potato production. According to a census compiled in the mid-nineteenth century, there were 5,256 farms in Suffolk County, and 97 percent of those farms grew potatoes, which led to a production increase that rose from 0.5 million bushels in 1840 to 3.5 million bushels in 1910.

Suffolk County farmers were always eager to adopt techniques to maximize use of the rich fertile soil of eastern Long Island. The early settlers learned from the Native Americans who originally inhabited the area that the decaying bodies of menhaden, an oily forage fish, spread out onto the soil was an excellent fertilizer. This was one part of the commercial menhaden industry that spanned over 150 years.[11] Later, modern fertilizer products were introduced.

As the agricultural industry became more commercialized, methods were developed to improve and expand on farming operations. In 1888, Daniel Hallock invented a crude mechanical potato digger and later developed a weeding device to greatly increase potato production. In 1938, H.R. Telmedge, a farmer from Riverhead, installed the first farming irrigation system in New York State. Before that, farmers depended entirely on rainwater for their farming needs.[12] The first use of pesticides, like the poisonous Paris Green, began to be used in abundance by the early 1900s, via horse-drawn sprayers, to combat ravenous insects that were causing disastrous effects on the crops. In 1946, DDT began to be used. This highly toxic pesticide was described at the time as the "nearly perfect control of potato insects." Unfortunately, the effect on the soil, drinking water and surrounding wildlife caused by high levels of harmful contaminants from these pesticides was not discovered until years later.

A promotional vehicle used by the Nassau and Suffolk Farm Bureaus in 1948 with the slogan "Eat Long Island Potatoes." *Courtesy of the Water Mill Museum.*

Along with production efforts, local farmers engaged in a robust advertising campaign. In 1895, one local newspaper article stated, "The potato crop as you all know is and has been for years the most important crop of this end of Long Island, in fact I believe there are as many acres devoted to this crop as to all other cultivated crops."[13] In 1916, a group of Long Island farmers formed the Suffolk County Farm Bureau, an organization used to advance their collective agricultural interests.[14] Later, industry officials embarked on an improved advertising campaign showcased by a potato-shaped automobile adorned with a slogan that read "Eat Long Island Potatoes."

Ultimately, the potato would make Suffolk County one of the one hundred richest counties in the United States in farm income. In fact, of the three thousand counties in the United States, Suffolk County was ranked second in potato production.[15] By 1943, the county maintained fifty-five thousand acres of potatoes and thirteen thousand acres of other crops, such as cauliflower, string beans and a variety of fruit. According to the 1945 Potato-Harvest survey, nearly 20 percent of the ninety-eight million bushels of potatoes harvested from the three largest potato growing states in the eastern United States came from Long Island's seventy thousand acres of potatoes.[16] In 1949, the county was estimated to have produced between fourteen million and eighteen million bushels of potatoes.

48,000 acres in Nassau and Suffolk Counties produce high quality Long Island Potatoes

Potato harvest on Long Island in 1930. Later, tractors and other machinery were added, which vastly increased the production of crops. *Courtesy of the Nassau County Department of Parks Recreation and Museums, Nassau County Photo Archive Center.*

The potato harvest generally began in August and ended in late November. Steel machinery was used to dig up the earth, and massive numbers of potatoes would fall back to the ground, where workers moved along the field, either bent over or crawling on their knees, to retrieve the crop and place them into baskets. As was the case with most types of farm labor, this backbreaking work was called stoop labor. Later, large potato combines were used to dig and then lift the seemingly endless crop up a chute, where workers would discard the vines and any other debris from the potatoes that would fall into large compartments in the trucks.

Once harvested, the potatoes were stored in sheds or barns through the winter to be readied for delivery the following spring. In the town of Cutchogue, a large building known as the Big Barn was constructed in 1927 and was used for nearly a century to store large numbers of potatoes. In some cases, potatoes were loaded onto trucks and driven to nearby processing plants. Here, laborers toiled in several large commercial grading sheds owned

11,500,000 bushels of Long Island
Potatoes are produced annually

By 1940, Long Island farms produced an estimated 11.5 million bushels of potatoes annually. *Courtesy of the Nassau County Department of Parks Recreation and Museums, Nassau County Photo Archive Center.*

Potato harvesting on Long Island in 1950. *Courtesy of the Nassau County Department of Parks Recreation and Museums, Nassau County Photo Archive Center.*

Opposite, top: A migrant farmworker picking strawberries near Hammond, Louisiana, in 1939. *Courtesy of the Library of Congress.*

Opposite, bottom: Farmworkers picking beans in Belle Glade, Florida, in 1937. All of the workers are seen bending or kneeling to pick the crops, thus earning the nickname "stoop labor." *Courtesy of the Library of Congress.*

Above: Farmworkers picking cantaloupes in the Imperial Valley, California, 1937. *Courtesy of the Library of Congress.*

by companies like I.M. Young and Agway, where they sized, washed, bagged and loaded potatoes into railway cars or trucks for delivery.[17] The smallest potatoes, called Bs, were separated and sold to soup and knish makers. The medium-sized potatoes were bagged and stacked on large pallets and sent to consumers. The largest potatoes, called chefs, were bagged and sold to specialty markets.

At the onset of World War II, the U.S. government placed heavy demands for potatoes on all agricultural areas, including Suffolk County, and even issued price supports to encourage the overproduction of potatoes in the country. However, once the war ended, the government was forced to buy large quantities of potatoes at fixed prices and, in some cases, paid farmers

This page: Migrant workers in a potato field. *Courtesy of the Records of the Migration Division, Archives of the Puerto Rican Diaspora, Centro de Estudios Puertorriquenos, Hunter College, City University of New York.*

to destroy any surplus crops. For reasons explained later in this book, potato production on Long Island began to decline steadily after World War II. However, above any other crop, it was the rise and fall of the potato that was intricately linked to the use of migrant farmworkers in Suffolk County.

DEMAND FOR LABOR

World War II created a serious demand for manpower in the country's armed services and military industries. This national call to service was answered by many Americans. As a result, a labor shortage was created in the agricultural industry, which was problematic to a nation at war. Farming communities in places like Suffolk County struggled to find enough help to harvest the staggering quantity of potatoes and other crops that were produced each year.

To address the nationwide farm labor shortage, President Franklin D. Roosevelt issued an executive order in 1942, known as the Emergency Farm Labor Program, or the Bracero program, which ultimately allowed millions of Mexican farmworkers to come to work on U.S. farms.[18] Over time, the country's reliance on migrant labor became entrenched. Laurence I. Hewes III, a retired attorney who served as counsel on the subcommittee on Migratory Labor in 1961, explained that a well-rooted stream of migrant workers had developed in three specific regions in the country. The first was the West Coast region, where workers flocked to the Imperial Valley in California, which produced roughly 80 percent of the nation's vegetables. The second was the Midwest region, which spans from Texas to Canada and produced the majority of wheat for the nation. The last region, which is the most relevant in this book, was the East Coast region, which spans from Florida to Maine, producing a variety of crops from potatoes to apples.

During the war, the farm labor shortage throughout New York continued to worsen. In 1942, Suffolk County alone faced a shortage of approximately 2,700 farm laborers.[19] One year later, New York State governor Thomas Dewey delivered a broadcasted speech that addressed the seriousness of the problem not only for New York but also for the national war effort.[20] "How are we going to provide food for our armed forces, for the people of our State and also for the starving millions whom our fighting men will surely rescue?" he asked. "We are going to help raise and harvest that food, each of us, according to his capacity. We are going to turn out and do the job—or

Farmworkers off in the distance picking cabbage on a large swath of land in the Imperial Valley, California, 1937. *Courtesy of the Library of Congress.*

we will go hungry. Worse than that, our armies and our allies will go hungry. No hungry nation, no hungry armies can win a war."

Governor Dewey announced a plan to recruit and train thirty thousand farmworkers throughout New York State.[21] He also coordinated with the United States employment offices to encourage all applicants to consider performing farm work in New York. Locally, all options were considered to address the labor shortage. Farmers sought to employ college and high school students who signed up for summer work, along with members of the Boy Scouts.[22] However, the task of transporting student laborers to and from the farms proved to be quite problematic. Moreover, since potatoes were harvested in the early fall, when schools were typically back in session, the use of student farm laborers was simply not feasible.

In 1943, Suffolk County announced a plan to hire Chinese immigrants living in New York City to work the farms.[23] One year later, approximately 160 German prisoners of war who were being detained at Camp Upton were also used to perform farm labor and were paid an estimated fifty-five cents per hour.[24] With the passage of the Displaced Persons Act of 1948, Suffolk

County farmers began to employ hundreds of Polish immigrants who were displaced by World War II.[25] Later, the Suffolk County Farm Bureau lobbied Governor Rockefeller to pass a law that would enable workers as young as twelve to perform limited farm work.[26] By 1953, local help still lagged, with only a small percentage of the county's 350,000 residents working on its 2,187 farms.[27] Thus while all viable options were continuously explored, a sustainable solution to the problem had not yet been found.

Desperate for help, the Suffolk County Farm Bureau lobbied the government for assistance. In response, the U.S. government contracted with the island of Jamaica to enlist more than four hundred farmworkers on short-term visas to supply the much-needed labor for the upcoming harvest.[28] The Jamaican workers were paid an average of forty cents per hour and came highly recommended because of their agricultural experience in working on sugar and banana plantations. They began working on Long Island in 1943 and were widely praised for their extraordinary work ethic and production.

Toward the end of the harvest season, representatives of the Jamaican government made demands for higher wages for their farmworkers.[29] Local farmers opposed the request, even if the loss of these workers would once again leave them with a labor shortage problem. As a result, the Jamaican farmers left the country at the end of the harvest, and the prospect of their return was unclear.[30] Despite the stalemate, approximately six hundred Jamaican workers returned the next year to work on Suffolk County farms.[31]

In 1947, Congress began to wind down the wartime emergency labor program and announced that it would no longer defray the transportation costs for the Jamaican farmworkers. As a result, Long Island farmers abandoned the use of Jamaican farmworkers and once again sought other options.[32] The Suffolk County Farm Bureau then contacted Puerto Rico, which, a few years earlier, had announced Operation Bootstrap, an economic initiative to help boost the island's economy. After several discussions, an agreement was reached that would send farm laborers from Puerto Rico to Long Island. On July 8, 1948, a DC-3 plane carrying approximately twenty-seven Puerto Rican men landed at MacArthur Field in Suffolk County.[33] They were the first of hundreds more Puerto Rican farmworkers who would later arrive to work on the farms of Long Island.[34]

Suffolk County farmers also began to employ an increasing number of Black farmworkers from southern U.S. states to supply the much-needed manpower on the farms.[35] By 1960, there were an estimated 4,500 migrant workers in Suffolk County. Of that total, an estimated 3,500 were mostly

Black men and women from Arkansas, Florida, Georgia, Virginia and the Carolinas. The remaining workers were from Puerto Rico.[36]

Over the years, New York's reliance on migrant farmworkers would continue to grow. In 1961, approximately 22,000 migrant laborers came to the state annually to work the farms.[37] At migrant agriculture labor's peak, close to 7,000 migrant farmworkers toiled throughout Long Island.[38] Over the years, this number would decline. By 1972, the Suffolk County Labor Department estimated that 5,000 migrants worked in Suffolk County and approximately 1,600 resided in the area.[39] As with nearly all of the farming communities throughout the country, Suffolk County once struggled with a demand for labor that was ultimately addressed with the use of migrant farmworkers.

2

THE BIRTH OF AN ERA

LABOR LAWS

In 1935, the United States Congress enacted the National Labor Relations Act (NLRA).[40] This sweeping federal law protects the rights of employees, grants them the right to join labor unions, to engage in "protected, concerted activities to address or improve working conditions" and curtails labor practices that can harm the general welfare of workers, businesses and the U.S. economy. The National Labor Relations Board is an independent federal agency that was created to enforce the terms of the NLRA.

The NLRA covers most, but not all, employees. Most notably, and of great importance to this story, the law specifically excludes agricultural laborers.[41] As such, the very law intended to protect many employees in this country and allow them to join labor unions for job security and the betterment of working conditions does not apply to the farmworkers who help feed the nation. Without the protections of the NLRA, farmworkers were left without the force of a powerful federal agency and unable to engage in "protected, concerted activities."[42]

The agricultural exclusion from this federal labor law is perhaps the single most destructive force faced by the farmworkers of this nation. In 1969, Reverend Arthur Bryant of Greenport lambasted the exclusion when he told congressional leaders, "Both the National Labor Relations Act exclusion and the various State labor relations acts with their exclusions produced a serious problem for a democratic society. When a great bulk of our citizens had their unalienable rights of citizenship enhanced by the right of collective bargaining, those without the right became second-class citizens."[43] Burt Nueborne, a former attorney for the American Civil Liberties Union (ACLU), described this exclusion as one of the nation's greatest social failures and stated, "They took the most vulnerable part of the American labor force and threw them out of the lifeboat."[44]

In 1961, Senator Harrison Williams Jr., a New Jersey Democrat, proposed a federal bill that was tantamount to a "New Deal" to alleviate the living conditions of migrant farmworkers, which continued to worsen each year.[45] The bill offered financial benefits, public health programs, education and children's day care centers for areas where migrant laborers worked. Unfortunately, the bill did not gain any political traction. Joseph Monserrat, a chief of the Migrant Labor Division of the Puerto Rican government, also advocated to change the laws and to raise the federal minimum wage and have compulsory workmen's compensation for all agricultural workers.[46] Monserrat added, "I think it is something that should bother the conscious of the people that the workers who pick our food and fiber in 1961 can lose an arm or a leg and not collect a cent for it because there is no compensation, while their brothers in the industry can."

In New York, Section 701 (3) of the New York State Employment Relations Act also excluded farm laborers. For more than three decades, state legislators and advocates for migrant workers sought to change this provision without any success.[47] In 1969, Assemblyman Manuel Ramos (D-Bronx), who sponsored several bills seeking a change in the law, stated, "It seems like every state in the union is waiting for the federal government to take the lead." Reverend Arthur Bryant from Greenport collected more than four thousand signatures from the local community supporting this bill. Ultimately, the proposed bill failed to become law.

Across the country, Cesar Chavez, along with Delores Huerta, spearheaded a nonviolent movement to secure the rights of farmworkers to negotiate with farm owners in Delano, California. Together, they formed a labor union called the National Farm Workers Association (NFWA), engaged in a strike against local growers and a national boycott of grape products and went on a 250-mile trek from Delano to Sacramento to promote their cause. Chavez even went on a twenty-five-day hunger strike to support the movement. Over time, the NFWA movement gained support from national political figures, including Robert F. Kennedy.

After years of continuous pressure, the California Agricultural Labor Relations Act of 1975 passed into law. This landmark U.S. statute established the right to collective bargaining for farmworkers in California, a first in U.S. history. Sadly, it would take New York nearly half a century to finally pass a similar law. Moreover, since migrant farmworkers resided in other states, they were unable to vote in New York. This, along with the exclusion of rights under federal and state labor laws, left them completely disadvantaged and powerless to change their conditions.

Thus migrant farmworkers traveled from state to state without the support or protection of federal or state labor laws. This left them vulnerable to the rampant abuse and exploitation that would come to define the migratory labor system in many areas that were known for their agricultural output, including Suffolk County.

LABOR CAMP REGULATIONS

To accommodate the thousands of migratory farmworkers who were flowing into the state each year to work during the harvest seasons, New York implemented a series of employment and housing regulations. In 1946, New York passed the Migrant Registration Law, which required all employers, crew leaders and contractors who were expecting to employ, recruit or transport ten or more out-of-state migrant farm or food processing workers to register with the Department of Labor.[48] Later, the law was reduced to cover as few as five workers.[49]

Additional regulations governing the housing of migrant laborers were implemented in 1954 when Governor Thomas E. Dewey signed a bill into law to improve the living and working conditions of migrant farm workers in New York State.[50] Four years later, New York governor Averell Harriman announced a series of sweeping changes to the state's sanitary code, which regulates light, air, safety and fire hazards at migrant labor camps in the state.[51]

The updated law heavily regulated the use of portable kerosene heaters at labor camps, which was one of the leading causes of fires, and required that all heating devices be properly installed and maintained. The law also required labor camps to provide forty square feet of sleeping space for each occupant, along with hot and cold water for each camp that housed twenty-five or more migrant workers between October 1 and May 1 of each year. Additionally, all new buildings that housed fifteen or more people were required to be fireproof, have easily accessible emergency exits and be properly ventilated with comfortable temperatures in all rooms. Labor camps were also required to be structurally safe and have waterproof roofing and siding. Lastly, all camps were required to be monitored by a competent person who must perform periodic maintenance. State inspectors were empowered with the legal authority to revoke or suspend the operating licenses of camp operators who failed to comply with the law.[52]

Local ordinances were also updated to reflect the heightened governance over labor camps. In 1957, the Town of Southold announced general land use regulations for the first time in its 317-year history.[53] The town's rapid growth in population made it necessary to take steps to assure the "orderly, healthful and planned use of land." The newly formed zoning ordinance in Southold governed the formation and usage of migrant labor camps in the township in accordance with all applicable laws. In an effort to preserve the integrity of nearby homes, the ordinance restricted all farm labor camps from being situated nearer to any other residence than the residence of the grower operating the camp.

These sweeping regulations in New York were intended to ensure a safe and adequate living space for all of the thousands of migrant workers flowing into the state each year. Unfortunately, as it will be shown, many camp operators in Suffolk County either failed or outright refused to adhere to these stringent laws, and their noncompliance had dire consequences to the farmworkers who occupied the labor camps.

A NEW ERA

In 1942, the New York State Farm Security Administration first announced that mobile low-cost migratory labor camps were permissible in the upstate counties of Wayne and Niagara and the Long Island counties of Nassau and Suffolk.[54] While this appeared to be the break that the labor-needy Long Island growers hoped for, there were several procedural hurdles that had to be cleared. Prospective labor camp owners were first required to gain approval of such plans from their respective townships. Growers seeking to operate a labor camp were also required to form a cooperative, or corporation, and register the camps with the county. They also had to establish prevailing wages for the workers and provide transportation to and from the various farms.

In these early years, proposals for labor camps were met with stubborn resistance from residents throughout Suffolk County who stood opposed to migrant laborers working and residing in their towns. In 1942, the Riverhead Town Board rejected a proposal to establish a migrant labor camp to accommodate up to five hundred farmworkers two miles northwest of Riverhead village.[55] A similar proposal for a labor camp in Southampton was also rejected.

Racial animosity appeared to be a strong factor in the public's dissent. In Southold, when a group of growers proposed the establishment of a labor camp in 1943, the residents there strongly opposed the notion of having "several hundred colored men from the South to work in Suffolk."[56] A short time later, a new resolution was met with resistance for the same reason. Realizing that the proposal was doomed to fail again, the growers conditioned the passage of the new resolution on using laborers exclusively from within New York State. Given the constant struggle to find enough local help to work the farms, the growers must have known that using only in-state labor would not fully satisfy their needs. Nevertheless, they agreed to settle on this proposal, and the Town of Southold approved the establishment of labor camps.

However, throughout Suffolk County, opposition to labor camps continued for the next several years. In 1946, the residents of Wading River and Shoreham thwarted a proposal to purchase a tract of land to erect a labor camp approximately four miles from the center of each town.[57] Former town attorney Lester M. Emmett led a delegation in opposition to the proposed labor camp. "We have a large number of objections to having a migrant farm labor camp at our back door," declared Emmett. "If the camp were established at that location during the summer months the farm laborers, among whom there might be a very undesirable element, would be overrunning the beaches of Wading River and Shoreham." Emmett also relayed the residents' concerns over the effect of migrant children on the local school systems and overall safety of the community.

One year later, hundreds of Calverton residents opposed the establishment of a labor camp in their town.[58] Citing similar concerns, the petition objected to bringing a "transient population" that would leave the town with "crime, disease and undesirable persons." In 1954, a large group of Peconic residents attended a public meeting and vigorously opposed a plan by Long Island Produce & Fertilizer Company to erect a labor camp in that town.[59] Two years later, more than one hundred residents from Yaphank signed a petition opposing the proposed enhancements at the McKasty labor camp in their town.[60] The firestorm erupted in the community when the camp owner purchased a prefabricated housing unit designed to be a home for war veterans and began construction without the required permit to enlarge his labor camp.

Over the years, public opposition to the establishment of migrant labor camps throughout Suffolk County began to wane. Specific information that would explain this shift could not be located. However, it is very likely that sympathies over the national pressure placed on the agricultural industry, both during World War II and its aftermath, led to the softening opposition. Also, since these were residents of deeply rooted farming communities, it is likely that they accepted labor camps as an unavoidable solution and acceded to their construction in their townships. Ultimately, once these procedural hurdles were satisfied, the era of the migrant labor camps in Suffolk County was born.

In June 1943, the Suffolk County Farm Bureau announced the anticipated opening of four labor camps to be used to house approximately 400 farmworkers from the island of Jamaica. The first of these camps was a large three-story frame cottage called Lake Lodge in the hamlet of Peconic, which was used to house approximately 100 Jamaican farmworkers.[61] A short time later, approximately 160 Jamaican farmworkers were housed at the Edwin Gould Foundation Camp in Kings Park, and the remaining workers were housed at the former site of Gordan Hospital in Port Jefferson and on the grounds of a former mansion in Greenport.

Over the next few years, migrant labor camps began to spring up all over Suffolk County, with the labor force initially consisting of foreign workers from Jamaica and the Bahamas, and then Puerto Rican farmworkers, before shifting almost entirely to Black farmworkers from the South. In 1951, there were 29 registered camps.[62] By 1958, the number of camps in the county had ballooned to 134, which housed nearly 2,400 migrant workers.[63] According to a 1960 map prepared by the Suffolk County Department of Planning, there were 120 labor camps in the county's ten townships.[64] This appears to have been the peak period for labor camps, because as time went on, and for reasons explained later in this book, the number of camps began to decrease.[65]

Less than a decade later, the number of labor camps had reduced dramatically. By 1968, there were an estimated eighty-seven labor camps in Suffolk County, which housed nearly 1,300 migrant workers.[66] In 1975, there were approximately sixty-eight camps remaining.[67] Ten years later, there were approximately forty-five registered camps still operating in the county.[68] Today, there are a handful of labor camps remaining in Suffolk County. However, the structural conditions of these camps, along with the

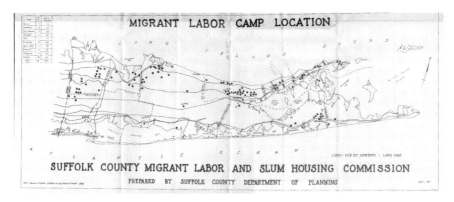

Migrant Labor Camp Location map created in 1960 by the Suffolk County Migrant Labor and Slum Housing Commission. Each dotted mark denotes the location of a labor camp in the county. At the time that this map was created, there were 120 labor camps in Suffolk County that housed nearly two thousand migrant farmworkers. *Courtesy of the Southold Historical Society, Southold, New York.*

many socioeconomic factors faced by those who inhabit them, are vastly different than they were during the mid-twentieth century.

During this peak era, the types of physical structures that housed migrant laborers varied widely. Typically, the larger labor camps consisted of army barracks and small cabin-style units. However, there were many other types of structures of varying size and type that served as migrant housing facilities. In most cases, these included shacks, rundown buildings, private homes, old barns, converted chicken coops, trailers, storage units and abandoned structures. Even the site of a historic mansion in Greenport and lake cottage in Peconic were used as labor camps.[69] Given the wide variety of migrant housing in Suffolk County, the term *labor camp* was used interchangeably at the time and will be similarly used throughout this book.

Migrant labor camps were most often situated in isolated rural or industrial areas adjacent to farms, warehouses and potato grading sheds and near train tracks or side roads. Such isolation gave the camps an aura of mystery. However, local news reporters were well aware of their existence. They periodically traveled from Riverhead to Greenport, on a tour of the so-called "Migrant Alley," reporting the deplorable conditions of the camps and the mistreatment of the migrant farmworkers who resided there. One reporter who toured several labor camps in 1952 stated, "Shoved off in the back country were migrant shacks that have no plumbing or indoor cooking facilities, that house up to 60 men, women and children, that swarm with flies and are slick with grease."[70]

Local reporter Harvey Aronson was one of the first reporters to frequently visit these camps. He once wrote, "Long Island poverty is at its rural worst in the potato-belt country of Suffolk East End, where the migrant labor system has left southern Negroes piled up in year-round shanty towns. They are places where curs, cats and children are unkept and underfoot; broken windows are blocked with newspapers and front yards are decorated with rusted automobiles and inoperative washing machines."[71] Throughout the years, the conditions of these camps worsened, which had wide-ranging adverse effects on the camp inhabitants and those in the surrounding communities. The following chapter identifies and details many of the labor camps that existed in Suffolk County.

3

THE LABOR CAMPS

THE CUTCHOGUE LABOR CAMP

The largest and unquestionably most notorious migrant labor camp in Suffolk County was the Cutchogue labor camp. Situated on Cox Lane between County Road 48 and Oregon Road, this camp existed for nearly four decades. Over the years, the camp had continued growth in size, had an on-site school for migrant children, was referenced for its deplorable conditions in two documentaries and was the scene of a horrific fire that claimed the lives of several migrant workers. To get a true picture of the Cutchogue labor camp, it is best to start at the beginning.

On June 12, 1944, a large group of growers from Southold and Shelter Island formed a corporation known as the Eastern Suffolk Cooperative.[72] According to records from the New York State Division of Corporations, the entity was described as a "Domestic Cooperative Corporation."[73] With its headquarters located in the hamlet of Peconic, the corporation was formed by growers who were concerned with the common good of their businesses.

Two years later, the Eastern Suffolk Cooperative purchased approximately three acres of land on Cox Lane in Cutchogue for approximately $1,000.[74] The cooperative also spent approximately $15,000 to purchase some army barracks, measuring twenty feet by one hundred feet, and three other structures, each measuring ten feet by twenty feet.[75] Small cabin-style units with corrugated aluminum roofs were also built at the camp. Later, military platform tents and additional barracks were also purchased, along with a large concrete block building with quarters that were used as office space for the management staff, rest and recreation rooms for the workers and a kitchen to allow for the supervised care of the children of the migrant workers. A small store, which sold a variety of goods, and an eatery called the Dixie Bell Inn were also added. Years later, the cooperative spent approximately $35,000 for a new men's dormitory. The fireproof cinder block building measured sixty-six feet by thirty-three feet and could accommodate nearly forty workers.[76] Ultimately, the camp was large enough to accommodate nearly three hundred farmworkers and was once touted in a local newspaper as a "model" labor camp in the state.[77] However, the occupants painted a far different and much bleaker picture of this labor camp.

Helen Wright Prince was a teacher of migrant children at the Cutchogue labor camp. In her memoir, titled *My Migrant Labor Camp School 1949–1961*, Prince described the setting of the camp, stating, "They formed a small one-street village of double-banked barracks and cabins, fenced from the road by barbed wire, unpainted, closed-packed, drab and colorless. No grass, just sand, weeds and mangy looking oaks surrounded by lovely woods."

Prince also explained the deplorable conditions she experienced at the camp's school. In the early years, she and her students had to endure the putrid stench of raw sewage leaking from a pipe just outside the door of the space that was used as a classroom. On one occasion, a space heater nearly exploded as she tried to ignite it, leaving soot on her face and neck. Prince often complained about the conditions of the camp school to George Seltzer, president of the Eastern Suffolk Cooperative and head trustee, who responded, "But Helen, you don't have to teach them anything. You just have to keep order!"[78] Prince lamented over the callous indifference that the camp owners had for the education of the children and stated, "At times, I was sure I was the only person in the whole U.S.A. who cared whether these children learned to read and write and love their neighbors."[79] Over the years, there were some improvements in the school, until its eventual closure in 1961, but despite Prince's noble efforts, such an environment was clearly not an ideal educational setting.

As time went on, the worsening conditions at the camp began to draw negative attention. In 1957, Albert Seay, president of the eastern Long Island branch of the National Association for the Advancement of Colored People (NAACP), publicly charged that the camp lacked sanitary facilities for the workers. Seay also claimed that the migrant workers were crowded into "filthy shacks with dirty linen" and were forced to pay overinflated

Helen Wright Prince in class with children of migrant farmworkers at the Cutchogue labor camp in Cutchogue, New York. Mrs. Prince taught at the school from 1949 to 1961, and she continually urged for improved conditions at the camp school. *Courtesy of the Southold Historical Society, Southold, New York.*

prices for basic food items. If workers bought food outside the camp, Seay explained, they would be penalized by not getting any work. In response to the allegations, Governor Harriman ordered hearings into what he described as the "dark, filthy hovels."[80] Eddie Clark, a migrant farmworker who once lived at the camp, stated, "It was a hellhole. A bunch of shabby cabins up next to each other."[81]

In 1960, Edward R. Murrow aired a documentary on CBS News titled *Harvest of Shame*. It chronicled the East Coast stream of migrant workers

This page: Inside the living quarters at the Cutchogue labor camp in 1947. Notice the scattered debris, uninsulated walls and dirty bedding. *Courtesy of the Southold Historical Society, Southold New York.*

A young child standing in the middle of the unpaved main road, also called Main Street, at the Cutchogue labor camp in Cutchogue, New York, in 1947. The large barracks can be seen at the rear right of the photo, and toward the front right of the photo, the roof of each cabin is covered by tents. *Courtesy of the Southold Historical Society, Southold, New York.*

who traveled northward from Florida up through New York and the West Coast stream of migrant workers throughout the U.S.-Mexico border. The film was intended to alert and, more importantly, shame the nation about the deplorable conditions faced by the migrant workers who helped feed the population of the "best fed country on earth." In the film, Murrow states, "We present this report on Thanksgiving because were it not for the labor of the people you are going to meet, you might not starve, but your table would not be laden with the luxuries that we have all come to regard as essentials." This documentary highlighted the poor treatment that farmworkers throughout the country were forced to endure. The Cutchogue labor camp was referenced in this documentary.

One year later, a fire tore through the camp, killing four migrant farmworkers and causing an estimated $25,000 in damages. In the aftermath of that fire, Suffolk County executive Lee Dennison stated, "The improvement of conditions for the migrant laborer must be undertaken by the county. If local governments will not take steps, we

Opposite: A large group of migrant workers gathered inside the Cutchogue labor camp in Cutchogue, New York, in 1947. One worker is entertaining the group by playing a violin. *Courtesy of the Southold Historical Society, Southold, New York.*

Above: A small store at the Cutchogue labor camp in Cutchogue, New York, which sold a variety of goods typically at overinflated prices, circa 1960s. *Courtesy of the Southold Historical Society, Southold, New York.*

must."[82] Harvey Aronson visited the camp on several occasions, searching for any improvements since the fire. He found none and instead described the harrowing scene as follows:

> *The macadam road curves through the camp like a scimitar—slicing past the single men's barracks and the family barracks, mostly long, gray buildings with green vents. The road goes past the big old donated television set, which is protected by a red blanket during the day, and the crisscrossing clotheslines. And it moves by the latrine-and-shower rooms, where there are even separate places for men and women and the sign is misspelled "Ladeis," and the clean, white-painted childcare center with its fenced-off play area. On the way out, the road curves past grass and weeds that have grown over once-blackened earth where a fire destroyed a barracks and killed four men in 1961.*[83]

A promotional advertisement created by the Eastern Suffolk Cooperative, Cutchogue, New York, circa 1953. Although it was once touted as a "model" labor camp, it ultimately received widespread notoriety for its poor living conditions and mistreatment of migrant farmworkers. *Courtesy of the Cutchogue New Suffolk Free Library.*

A volunteer of the Volunteers in Service to America (VISTA), Joseph Daugherty, lived at the camp for one harvest season in 1966 and provided much-needed assistance to the migrant workers. Daugherty later described the abysmal conditions of the camp. "In the area where I worked as a volunteer," he stated, "we found about eight toilets for 60–70 men and every morning seven of the eight toilets were stopped up." He also described the living quarters as "cabins with no cooking or heating facilities, bad sanitary conditions, and containing two or three small rooms for eight or ten people."[84]

Despite the growing notoriety, little was publicly known about the Cutchogue labor camp. However, that all changed in 1968 with the airing of a documentary titled *What Harvest for the Reaper?*[85] This jarring, one-of-a-kind production remains the only known footage of the grim conditions inside the infamous Cutchogue labor camp. The film also provided an unrivaled look at how the migrant workers were exploited by their crew leader, Andrew Anderson.

The aftermath of the October 8, 1961 fire at Cutchogue labor camp, which claimed the lives of James Davis, Charles Jordan, Leroy McKoy and James Overstreet and caused an estimated $25,000 in damages. *Courtesy of the Southold Historical Society, Southold, New York.*

What Harvest for the Reaper? was produced by Morton Silverstein and first aired on January 28, 1968. The film shows the large multiple occupancy sleeping quarters, also known as bullpens, where the men at the camp slept. Each man was given an average of forty square feet of living space, which is approximately the size of the top of a pool table. Although this was compliant with the sanitary code, by comparison, non-migrants enjoyed double that amount of living space. "This has been a major factor in the dehumanization of the farm laborer," declared Reverend Arthur Bryant from Greenport.[86] The code also required each bunk, bed, mattress, spring and pillow to be in good condition and every sheet and blanket to be cleaned. However, the bedding shown in the film did not appear to meet those requirements.

Throughout the documentary, the camp always appears to be in disrepair. In particular, most of the bathrooms were not functioning, a common complaint made by many, including VISTA volunteer Joseph Daugherty two years before the making of this film. Inoperative restroom facilities are severely problematic for a camp that ordinarily housed hundreds of workers throughout the season. At one point, thirty-eight men were forced to share only one operational bathroom. Reverend Arthur Bryant recalled an instance in which one of the few functional toilets was clogged for four days. With no repair in sight, he visited the Suffolk County Department of Health, sat on the desk of one of the inspectors and refused to leave until the department dispatched someone to ensure that repairs were made.

Representatives from the Eastern Suffolk Cooperative were also interviewed in the film. They arrogantly blamed the camp conditions on the migrant workers. One board member callously stated, "I think it's very unfair for us as board members to be nursemaids to these people. If they wish to live in filth, not wash and go to the bathroom in their own living quarters, there's no way I can stop it if I'm home in my own clean, lily-white sheets, which I change weekly." In response, Reverend Bryant aptly warned, "If we are going to say that the health of an industry is more important than the value of a human life, then this can sort of catch on and encompass all of us. We have to be concerned with him because 'he' is us." The lack of empathy and refusal to accept any responsibility by the trustees of the cooperative partially explains how the conditions of the camp were allowed to worsen over the years.

With operating costs continuing to rise, the Eastern Suffolk Cooperative applied for a special exception in 1966 with the town's Building Zoning Ordinance, seeking permission to replace the barracks with cement block fireproof housing units.[87] Once approved, the group then applied for a federal grant in the amount of $66,000 to pay for the improvements. However, the application, which was sponsored by Senator Robert F. Kennedy and Reverend Arthur Bryant, was denied because such grants were only available to nonprofit community organizations. As a result, the improvement plans were scrapped.[88] Later that year, the cooperative abruptly announced the closure of a state-run childcare center that served approximately forty migrant children at the camp between the ages of two and five.[89] The program was mostly funded by the state and offered the children supervised games, snacks and cots for afternoon naps. When pressed for a reason for the closing, William Chudiak, a trustee of the Eastern Suffolk Cooperative, claimed that it was because of a need to convert that area into a cooking space for the migrant workers.

Over the years, conditions at the camp continued to worsen, and violations began to mount. In 1970, the camp was denied a new permit and was ordered to be closed by the Department of Health.[90] The camp apparently reopened a short while later, and records of activity, albeit on a much smaller

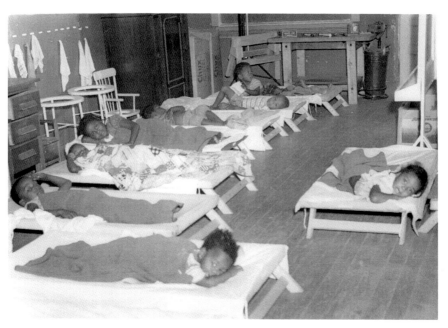

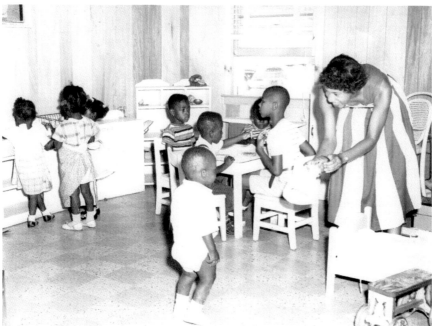

This page: Children in the childcare center at the Cutchogue labor camp. The center was largely funded by New York State and provided supervised games, snacks and cots for afternoon naps for the children of migrant workers, until it was abruptly closed in 1966, purportedly to make room for a new cooking space. *Courtesy of the Southold Historical Society, Southold, New York.*

scale, do indicate that the camp operated until at least 1975. Then, on May 9, 1983, the Eastern Suffolk Cooperative sold the land to a group called Prime Purveyors, who in turn constructed a warehouse on the property for dry goods.[91] Finally, on June 5, 1984, the Eastern Suffolk Cooperative formally dissolved nearly forty years after the day it first formed. According to New York State records, after the payment of all debts and expenses, the corporation had a surplus of $51,459.56, which was distributed equitably among the few remaining corporate officers.

The Cutchogue labor camp was once touted as a "model" camp that was required to solve the labor shortage in this rich agricultural region. However, through the years, it was plagued by poor and worsening conditions, mistreatment of migrant workers and the site of a fire that claimed four lives. Moreover, the camp operators appeared to have an indifferent, and at times hostile, attitude toward the inhabitants of the camp. As such, this camp can only be remembered for the notoriety it indeed deserves.

The Greenport Labor Camp

Situated approximately eight miles east of the Cutchogue labor camp, the Eastern Suffolk Cooperative operated another large labor camp at the site of the former Richard Conklin Mansion in Greenport.[92] Built in 1862, the mansion was a massive two-story building adorned with a captain's walk, ginger bread decorations, a cupola and five brick fireplaces.[93] The grounds of the mansion were part of the Sound View Stock Farm, which raised prized Thoroughbred horses, including Rarus, one of the country's leading racehorses at the time. After Conklin's death, the mansion was used as a clubhouse for the adjoining Kerwin Golf Course and would later become the site of the Greenport labor camp that accommodated as many to two hundred farmworkers at a time.

Edwin H. King, a prominent farmer from Orient, was instrumental in the establishment of the Greenport labor camp. In 1943, King wrote an editorial in a local newspaper urging Southold residents to approve plans to establish a government-sponsored labor camp at the site of the Conklin mansion.[94] The plan was twice rejected by town residents, along with Greenport mayor John F. Kluge and other town officials.[95] Undeterred, King consulted with federal and state agricultural officials and then purchased the forty-eight-acre Kerwin Golf Course, including the building, which he leased to the

RESIDENCE OF R.B.CONKLIN, GREENPORT, SUFFOLK CO.LI, N.Y.

A sketch of the Richard Conklin mansion in Greenport, New York. Built in 1862, the mansion was a part of the Sound View Stock Farm, which raised prized Thoroughbred horses, including Rarus, one of the country's leading racehorses at the time. After Mr. Conklin's death, the mansion was used as a club house for the adjoining Kerwin golf club and would later become the site of the Greenport labor camp, which accommodated as many as two hundred farmworkers at a time. The mansion was located on the North Road just east of Chapel Lane in Greenport, New York. *Courtesy of the Southold Free Library.*

government for a fee of one dollar per year for the duration of World War II. King also purchased two or three army barracks from Camp Upton and had them towed to the site to establish the labor camp.[96] After World War II, King leased the same property to the Eastern Suffolk Cooperative to operate the camp for a period of seven years before selling it to the group in 1952.

Information on the Greenport labor camp is scarce. However, it is known that, unlike the Cutchogue labor camp, this one housed only single men. The building's first floor was renovated to include a camp office, kitchen, canteen and mess hall. Near the main building, several one-story barracks were constructed for sleeping quarters, along with a recreation center.[97] Predating the Cutchogue labor camp, the Greenport camp was reportedly first used in 1943, when it housed approximately one hundred Jamaican farmworkers.[98] In ensuing years, hundreds of Bahamian, Jamaican, Puerto Rican, Mexican and Black American workers were housed at the Greenport camp.[99] Polish laborers who later arrived as part of the Displaced Persons Act of 1948 were also housed at this camp.[100]

The only known photographs of the Greenport labor camp, dated October 19, 1950, at the site of the former Richard Conklin mansion in Greenport, New York. The camp first opened in 1943 and operated until 1966. The top photo shows the former Richard Conklin mansion, and the bottom photo shows the labor camp structures that were erected on the grounds of the property. *Courtesy of Southold Free Library.*

In the summer of 1947, the Greenport labor camp housed more than two hundred Mexican workers who had previously worked the sugar beet harvest in Colorado and Montana.[101] During this time, nearly all of the Mexican farmworkers engaged in a one-day strike to demand higher wages.[102] A hearing, which was presided over by county official Walter G. Been and other state officials, was held in nearby Peconic to resolve the matter. Representatives from the Eastern Suffolk Cooperative argued that the workers, who were being paid sixty cents per hour, or six dollars per ten-hour day, were paid correctly, given their level of skill. The wage board agreed and ruled unanimously in favor of the growers. The Mexican workers, who had no representation at the hearing, reluctantly returned to work in the fields the next day. Despite being unable to secure higher wages, this extraordinary display of solidarity was rare for workers at any migrant labor camp on Long Island or in New York State.

The camp was later managed by a man named Harry Ambs for approximately ten years. During his tenure, the camp doubled in size. He reportedly arranged for transportation for the workers to attend church services in their native language and created recreational activities for them. One such event occurred in the summer of 1958, when the Westbury Society of Friends and the Eastern Suffolk Cooperative sponsored a softball tournament between the migrant workers at the Cutchogue labor camp and the workers at the Greenport labor camp.[103]

For two decades, the Greenport labor camp continued to operate, until it fell into disrepair and eventually closed. On April 3, 1966, the facility was destroyed by a premeditated fire at the request of the new owners, and the land was purchased and eventually used to create a nonprofit nursing, rehabilitation and adult day care home that still exists as of this writing.[104]

The North Fork

The labor camps operated by the Eastern Suffolk Cooperative in Cutchogue and Greenport were the largest in Suffolk County. For decades, they housed hundreds of American and foreign migrant farmworkers, and of the two, the Cutchogue camp certainly developed notoriety. However, throughout the twentieth century, there were well over 100 registered labor camps across the county, with a peak of 134 camps in 1958. By the late 1980s, most of the potato farms were gone and so were most of the labor camps. Regrettably, many of the documents pertaining to these labor camps have been discarded by various state agencies. However, the information found in various public records do shed light on some of the labor camps referenced throughout this chapter.[105]

The first documented labor camp in Suffolk County was located on the North Fork at a three-story cottage called Lake Lodge in the hamlet of Peconic. The camp opened in July 1943 and housed approximately one hundred Jamaican farmworkers. A short time later, three other camps opened in Greenport, Kings Park and Port Jefferson. Collectively, the four camps housed more than four hundred Jamaican farmworkers, all men who traveled to the United States from the island of Jamaica and then by train from New Orleans to Long Island. They were each paid $0.40 per hour for their labor and were lauded for being "virtually tireless" for working ten-hour days six days per week.[106] Local growers raised approximately $2,500 for upgrades to the camp, which included an outdoor latrine, a hot water heater and other related equipment.

Here, as was a common feature in most labor camps, the sleeping quarters for the workers was a bullpen-style room, and they all dined in a common mess hall. The camp's supervisor was a man named Carl Schleifer, who was a resident of Jamaica, and Walter I. Williams was the camp manager. Both men reportedly strived to provide recreational activities for the workers, including cricket, tennis and a variety of indoor games.

Lake Lodge in Peconic, New York, in 1949. Beginning in 1943, this building and the surrounding property was used as a labor camp to house approximately one hundred Jamaican farmworkers. It is believed to have been the first labor camp in Suffolk County. *Courtesy of the Southold Historical Society, Southold, New York.*

It is believed that the camp was in operation for several years, until 1947, when the U.S. government began to wind down its emergency wartime labor program and no longer contracted with the island of Jamaica for agricultural laborers. Despite its short tenure, the Lake Lodge labor camp remains an important part of this history as the first recorded labor camp in Suffolk County.

The North Fork's easternmost hamlet is Orient, and this area had always been known to be rich in agricultural production. Edwin H. King, the same farmer who was instrumental in establishing the Greenport labor camp, had for many years owned a seventy-acre parcel of farmland in Orient with a frontage of more than 1,400 feet overlooking the Long Island Sound.[107] Little has been documented about the King labor camp. However, it is believed that at this location, migrant workers were housed in various structures on the farm, including the original Orient schoolhouse building. Female workers slept on the first floor, and the male workers were housed in the upper attic area of the school building, which was only accessible by

Top: A group of Jamaican farmworkers picking beans on the Julius Sebroski farm in Southold, New York, in 1943. *Courtesy of the* North Fork Life, *July 1, 1943, Mattituck, New York.*

Middle: A group of Jamaican farmworkers dining in the mess hall at the Lake Lodge labor camp in Peconic, New York, in 1943. *Courtesy of the* North Fork Life, *July 1, 1943, Mattituck, New York.*

Bottom: Jamaican farmworkers at the Lake Lodge labor camp in Peconic, New York, in 1943. *Courtesy of the* North Fork Life, *July 1, 1943, Mattituck, New York.*

Left: The directors at the Lake Lodge labor camp in Peconic, New York, in 1943. On the left is camp supervisor Carl Schleifer, who was a resident of Jamaica. On the right is camp manager Walter I. Williams. *Courtesy of the North Fork Life, July 1, 1943, Mattituck, New York.*

Right: Two Jamaican farmworkers carrying baskets of string beans in 1943 at the Lake Lodge labor camp in Peconic, New York. *Courtesy of the North Fork Life, July 1, 1943, Mattituck, New York.*

a pull-down ladder inside the front doorway.[108] The potatoes harvested at this and other nearby farms were transported by ferry to Boston and other nearby cities.[109] After forty-eight years of farming in Orient, Edwin H. King announced his retirement and held an auction in 1961 to sell all of his remaining farm equipment and buildings.[110]

The Latham family in Orient also operated a labor camp that housed approximately thirty-five workers from Puerto Rico, as well as Black farmworkers from southern states who were recruited by a crew leader named Johnny Collins.[111] During an interview, Dan Latham once stated that these workers were able to pick between 100 and 120 bushels of potatoes each day, and many of them would return each year, including one man who worked in the area for thirty-three years. Other labor camps in Orient included Tabor labor camp and the Terry labor camp.

By 1960, Southold township had twenty-four registered migrant labor camps that housed an estimated 630 workers. This was the largest number of workers in the county. Some of these camps included the Krupski labor camp on Bridge Lane in Cutchogue, North Fork Nurseries in Jamesport, the Agway labor camp in Mattituck and the Duroski labor camp in Southold.

Top: Reverend William E. Greene of the Shiloh Baptist Church in Southold discusses religion with a group of Jamaican farmworkers at the Lake Lodge labor camp in 1943. *Courtesy of the North Fork Life, July 1, 1943, Mattituck, New York.*

Bottom: A group of Jamaican farmworkers performing laundry services in 1943 at the Lake Lodge labor camp in Peconic, New York. *Courtesy of the North Fork Life, July 1, 1943, Mattituck, New York.*

In 1966, Robert Bolling was granted a special exception to the local zoning law to operate a labor camp on Queen Street in Greenport, just two miles east from the large Greenport camp. This same camp was previously owned and operated by Len Jones, a Greenport resident known for a deformity that left him with one arm. Both Jones and Bolling were reportedly abusive to the migrant workers at the camp, and over the years, the camp received numerous violations, until its court-ordered closure in 1982. [112]

In 1986, a small group of growers formed the North Fork Packers Inc. and operated the I.M. Young labor camp on Depot Lane in Cutchogue. The cinder block building was located near railroad tracks and adjacent to

The original schoolhouse in Orient, New York, 1938. The schoolhouse was once located on the Edwin H. King farm and was reportedly used to house migrant farmworkers. In 1949, the schoolhouse was donated and relocated to the Oysterponds Historical Society, where it is used today for various historical exhibits. *Courtesy of the Oysterponds Historical Society, Orient, New York.*

a large potato storage shed, known locally as the Big Barn, which had been in use for eighty years. In the mid-1990s, the camp was operated by Carl Beamon, who was reputed to have beaten his workers with a thick stick or an iron skillet. Beamon rode along on his notorious red bus, a rusting heap that he used to recruit and transport migrant workers to Long Island each year.[113] The food he reportedly fed to his workers was little more than grits and pig parts.[114] "Beamon treated people like animals," said Walt Zilnicki, who once had to break a lock to the camp's office door to free Frank Singleton, a migrant worker who was forced to tend to Beamon's bedridden wife. "It was horrible back then," stated Zilincki.

After the death of Carl Beamon in 1998, James Wilson and Walter Zilnicki operated the camp until May 1, 2006, when the Big Barn was destroyed by a raging fire.[115] At the time, it was the last commercial potato shed in the area and served the few remaining potato growers.[116] As the fire raged on, James Wilson stated, "We've lost the barn. This is the last of it. We've lost everything." Thus after sixty years, the last of the migrant labor camps in

Eddie Clark riding on a potato planter at a farm in Cutchogue, New York, 1994. *Courtesy of the Lynn Johnson Collection, Mahn Center for Archives and Special Collections, Ohio University Libraries.*

A woman watching television inside a room at the I.M. Young Labor camp in Cutchogue, New York, 1994. On the right, Carl Beamon (*shirtless*) and another man are seated at the picnic table in another room. *Courtesy of the Lynn Johnson Collection, Mahn Center for Archives and Special Collections, Ohio University Libraries.*

Frank Bryant, a migrant farmworker from Alabama, taking a break after bagging potatoes at a grader in Cutchogue, New York, 1994. *Courtesy of the Lynn Johnson Collection, Mahn Center for Archives and Special Collections, Ohio University Libraries.*

Workers bagging potatoes at a potato grader in Cutchogue, New York, 1994. *Courtesy of the Lynn Johnson Collection, Mahn Center for Archives and Special Collections, Ohio University Libraries.*

Cutchogue finally closed for good. It should be noted, with great irony, that fire, which took so many innocent lives over the years at various labor camps, proved the death knell for the final labor camp from this era in this historic farming town.

Not all of the North Fork growers relied on the migrant labor camps to satisfy their labor needs. Families likes the Wickhams have always remained independent of the large cooperative farming groups, and for them, it has always been a family operation. The Wickham family has maintained a three-hundred-acre farm in Cutchogue since 1661. During the labor camp era, John Wickham steadily employed a small number of migrant farmworkers and provided adequate housing on his farm for them. He also strived to treat his workers fairly and with dignity and respect.[117]

Nathan Harris worked for Mr. Wickham for many years. Together, they developed a mutually respectful working relationship, and the men constructed a spring to form an irrigation pond. Harris eventually saved up enough money to purchase his own home in Cutchogue. John Wickham was also known to allow some migrant workers to fish from a fresh-water creek on his sprawling property. Frank Singleton, who suffered many abuses from various farmers and crew leaders, was one of the workers allowed to fish from the creek. He spoke very highly of Mr. Wickham and always appreciated this simple yet lasting gesture of hospitality.[118]

John Wickham died in 1994, and today, his son Tom Wickham still operates the same farm as his family has done for so many years. He, too, uses migrant laborers, mostly from Central America, as part of the H-2A Program under New York law. Like his father before him, Tom Wickham takes great pride in having a mutually respectful and long-lasting relationship with his workers. Sadly, the relationship that families like the Wickhams have shared with their farmworkers was the exception to the typically poor treatment of farmworkers housed in migrant labor camps throughout Suffolk County.

Fishers Island is located on the eastern entrance of the Long Island Sound and approximately two miles off the coast of Connecticut. Despite its location, Fishers Island is in New York State and a part of Southold township. Records reveal that there was also a labor camp on the island that used a small number of migrant workers for many years, which continued at least through 1968.

Each year from April to October, a small number of Black migrant workers traveled from Hobe Sound, Florida, to Fishers Island to perform primarily landscaping duties for residential estates on the island. These

workers were housed in a building on Crescent Avenue adjacent to the location where the workers were dispatched for work each day. The men were employed by Fisher Island Farms, an umbrella company that owned the utilities, a contracting company and various other businesses on the island. By 1965, the company was sold and became known as the Fisher Island Utility Company.

Opposite: Freshwater creek on the Wickham farm in Cutchogue, New York. John Wickham once gave permission to Frank Singleton and other migrant workers to fish from this creek. *Courtesy of Mark Torres.*

Above: A home for migrant workers on the Tom Wickham farm. The small portion in the front of the home (with a bicycle near the rear) is the original home that was constructed, and later it was expanded. *Courtesy of Mark Torres.*

Right: Tom Wickham on his farm in Cutchogue, New York. The Wickham family has been farming on this three-hundred-acre land since 1661. *Photo courtesy of Mark Torres.*

This page: A parcel of land on the Wickham farm in Cutchogue, New York. *Courtesy of Mark Torres.*

A 1950 aerial photo of Fishers Island looking east across the shuttered Fort H.G. Wright and the Elizabeth Field Airport. *Courtesy of H.L. Ferguson Museum, Fishers Island, New York.*

Jim Wall spent most of his life on Fishers Island and as a young man worked with the migrant workers. According to Mr. Wall, the workers were not recruited by a crew leader. Instead, they first came to the island after hearing about some available work, created a relationship with the company and continued to return each year. He recalled working with Dan Martin, George Sanders and Charlie Williams, all migrant workers from Florida. They each earned sixty cents per hour and were typically paid by check on Fridays that they were able to cash with the company. Sometimes, the workers came with their wives, but Mr. Wall had no recollection of them ever traveling to the island with children. He stated that the workers were generally treated well and were housed in a well-maintained building. He further added that a former military base on the island was used by the migrant workers, some of whom were domestic workers, for recreation and entertainment during their stay.

While the migrant workers on Fishers Island performed a vastly different type of work than the workers on the potato farms and processing plants of Suffolk County, and their labor camp operated differently than most camps of the time, the migrant labor camp on Fishers Island and the experiences of the workers who stayed there are an important part of this history.

The Fishers Island Labor Camp. This building, located on Crescent Avenue, on Fishers Island, New York, was used to house migrant workers from 1958 to 1968 to perform landscaping duties on the island. The building is now used for boat storage. *Courtesy of Pierce Rafferty.*

This photograph, taken on December 8, 2004, shows the former military building on Hound Lane, on Fishers Island, New York, which was used by migrant workers for recreation and entertainment. The building was later renovated and became the Fishers Island Community Center. *Courtesy of John Spofford.*

Riverhead

With thirty registered labor camps housing an estimated four hundred migrant workers, the town of Riverhead had the second-largest concentration of migrant workers and labor camps in Suffolk County in 1960. Here, labor camps were often situated in relatively close proximity to each other. On Osborne Avenue, there were several labor camps, including the Farmers Exchange, the H. Sacks & Sons labor camp, the I.M. Young labor camp and the Agway labor camp, which housed about twenty migrant workers in a barracks-style camp.[119] The Myron Nelson labor camp and the Riverside labor camp were both situated on Old Quogue Road. Other camps in the area included the Pollack labor camp on Edgar Avenue, the Bushwick labor camp on Railroad Avenue and a nearby camp operated by the Gallo Potato Grading Company.

On June 4, 1959, the Fargo Potato Company was formed and opened the Fargo labor camp on Laurel Lane in the hamlet of Laurel. This camp housed approximately thirty migrant laborers. One reporter who visited this camp described the morose setting in the bullpen as "beds lined up against a concrete wall which had few pillows and no linens. Each bed had a blanket and a stained mattress. A sign above the kitchen door read, "65 cents per meal."[120] Carlos Wright was once the crew leader of this camp. Standing at a massive six foot four and more than 250 pounds, Wright was known to be an intimidating figure. After thirty-six years, the Fargo labor camp closed, and the corporation was dissolved in 1995.

The Zahler labor camp was on Edgar Avenue in the hamlet of Aquebogue. One reporter who visited this camp noticed the dozen or so laborers who slept on layers of bunk beds, some double and some single, in filthy barracks with a broken television set arranged in the corner of the room. In 1969, Long Island congressman Allard Lowenstein toured this camp and noted the leaky roof without shingles and the rotted screen door at the entrance.[121] The heat inside the camp was oppressive, even with the windows open, which allowed a cool breeze to blow in. The bullpen had nearly two dozen cots, with no other furniture, and each bed had worn mattresses and thin blankets. The bathroom had two commodes, a sink and a shower. Water trickled from a leaky pipe, which left the floor muddy, and the room reeked of urine. One worker complained that he had not received more than thirty-seven dollars a week during the entire summer at the camp.

This page: Various labor camps used to house migrant farmworkers in the 1970s in Riverhead, New York. *Courtesy of Raymond Nelson.*

This page: An abandoned migrant labor camp on Edgar Avenue in Riverhead, New York. *Courtesy of Mark Torres.*

Opposite: The buildings that were once reportedly used for the Fargo labor camp in Laurel, New York. The camp operated from 1959 to 1995. The building on the right would have been used as the sleeping quarters for migrant workers, and the taller building would likely have been used to process potatoes and other crops. Today, the buildings are privately owned and used for storage. *Courtesy of Kathleen Goggins Nickles.*

Above: The train tracks adjacent to the potato processing building at the former Fargo Labor Camp. The proximity to the tracks allowed for the speedy transport of crops to and from the camp. *Courtesy of Kathleen Goggins Nickles.*

Before operating the I.M. labor camp in Cutchogue, Carl Beamon formed Beamon Produce Inc. and opened his own labor camp on Kroemer Avenue in Calverton. Beamon purchased the land in 1975 for $40,000 and oversaw the camp, which housed between ten and fifteen migrant men and women.[122] Over the years, Beamon received numerous violations, including a citation in 1990 for operating the camp without a permit. This camp appears to have closed by the mid-1990s, and records show that the corporation was dissolved by proclamation in 2001.[123]

Shelter Island

At just twenty-seven square miles, Shelter Island is a small, secluded island located between the North and South Forks. In 1652, the Sylvester Manor comprised the entire island and was established by the Dutch as a provisional plantation that used slave labor for the Barbadian sugar trade.[124] Over time, individual farmers were able to acquire parcels of land. In 1875, there were seventy-seven farms totaling 7,013 acres, mostly for subsistence farming. By 1940, there were twenty-two farms totaling 1,785 acres used mostly for commercial purposes. A few years later, a small group of growers formed the Shelter Island Farmer's Cooperative and named Sylvester Prime as its president. On August 22, 1950, the group opened the Beanery, a farm and factory plant that harvested lima beans and cauliflower.

The Beanery plant consisted of an ammonia compressor, dubbed Big Bertha, that was powered by a diesel engine with twenty-four-inch-diameter pistons.[125] At its peak, the plant was able to produce more than one million pounds of lima beans per season, packaged in eight-ounce, ten-ounce and two-pound packages, along with an estimated twenty tons of cauliflower. The vegetables were flash frozen and prepared for delivery to large companies, such as Libby's and Birds Eye.[126]

The Beanery employed approximately fifteen Black migrant laborers from Alabama and the Carolinas who were recruited by a crew leader named Williams and supervised by a former sea captain named Harold Jennings.[127] The work was strenuous, and the plant operated with large machinery, which was always dangerous. Approximately forty woman who resided on the island were also employed to perform the less dangerous work at the plant.

While some were housed in a building behind the facility, the majority of the migrant workers were housed in a camp approximately two miles from the Beanery plant.[128] During the workdays, some of the children of the migrant workers attended the school on Shelter Island. However, the workers spent nearly all of the time isolated at the camp. If any trouble arose, the lone policeman at the time, named Pete Hannabury, reportedly escorted those involved to the ferry with a one-way ticket off the island. A string of hurricanes in 1954 and an ensuing pestilence of insects devastated the crops on the island. This ultimately led to the closure of the Beanery, and most of the migrant workers returned to their homes. By 1960, there were two labor camps on the island that housed more than twenty migrant laborers, but information on these camps is scarce.

This page and following two pages: Migrant workers at the Beanery Plant on Shelter Island, New York. The plant opened in 1950 and processed lima beans and cauliflower which were flash frozen and sold to companies like Libby's and Birds Eye. Heavy machinery at the plant, including a large compressor dubbed Big Bertha with twenty-four-inch-diameter pistons, was dangerous to operate. Multiple hurricanes in 1954 and an ensuing insect pestilence led to the closure of the plant. *Courtesy of the Shelter Island Historical Society.*

An old barn that was reportedly used to house migrant workers in the 1960s on Menantic Road on Shelter Island approximately two miles from the site of the Beanery plant. *Courtesy of Mark Torres.*

THE SOUTH FORK AND WESTERN SUFFOLK COUNTY

Although fewer in number than its counterpart to the north, the South Fork also had labor camps. By 1960, the town of Southampton had thirteen registered migrant labor camps that housed approximately 260 workers. The camps here were typically just as filthy and dangerous. In December 1957, an overheated space heater caused a fire to sweep through the barracks at the A.C. Carpenter labor camp on Deerfield Road in Water Mill.[129] Within minutes, the wooden structure was a raging inferno, and the 25 migrant farm workers who were in the camp were fortunate to escape without injury. Several years later, a fire erupted at the Rosko labor camp on Butter Lane in East Hampton.[130] No injuries were reported. The Southampton Produce labor camp also operated in this area for approximately thirty years.

By 1960, there were two registered labor camps in East Hampton that housed approximately twenty-five farmworkers. One of these camps included the South Shore Produce labor camp in the hamlet of Wainscott.

This camp had been in operation for nearly fifty years before its closure in 2006. The town of Bridgehampton had several labor camps, including the Anthony Babinski labor camp on Mecox Road, the H. Sacks & Sons labor camp on Montauk Highway and the Wesnofske labor camp on Cooks Lane. The Baldwin labor camp was located on Foster Avenue and housed approximately thirty-one farmworkers. One of the most notorious labor camps in in Bridgehampton was the Jacobs labor camp. This single-story home on Foster Avenue was owned by Henry Jacobs and received numerous violations over the years. In 1968, a horrific fire claimed the lives of three migrant workers at this camp.

Labor camps also existed in the western part of Suffolk County. In 1943, U.S.–sponsored labor camps using hundreds of Jamaican farm laborers operated at the Edwin Gould Foundation Camp in Kings Park and at the former site of Gordan Hospital in Port Jefferson. By 1960, the town of Brookhaven had twenty registered camps that housed an estimated 314 workers. One of these camps included the Lohman Farm labor camp, which housed between 6 and 10 migrant farmworkers. Other camps in the township of Brookhaven included the Bruno Beck labor camp in Port Jefferson, the Stanley Detmers labor camp in East Setauket, the Peters

A building on Deerfield Road in Water Mill, New York, that was believed to have once been used by the Carpenter labor camp. To the rear and unseen in the photograph were two barns situated near railroad tracks, which allowed for the easy transport of potatoes and other crops. Today, the building is used for storage. *Courtesy of the Water Mill Museum.*

labor camp in Gordon Heights, the Nowaski labor camp in Miller Place and the Still Farm labor camp in Coram. The town of Smithtown had eight labor camps with about 85 farmworkers, Babylon had three labor camps with approximately 19 workers and Islip had one registered labor camp with 9 workers.

Lastly, the town of Huntington had seventeen labor camps that housed approximately 183 farmworkers. One of the camps here was the John Brigati labor camp. This camp was located on Old Country Road in Melville and generally housed between 6 and 13 migrant farmworkers. Over the years, this camp received several violations, including a citation on July 31, 1970, for operating the camp without a permit.

In some cases, camp operators housed migrant workers in private homes. In 1961, a predawn raid was conducted by building inspectors at a two-story home in East Northport. They found approximately thirty Puerto Rican migrant laborers sleeping in cramped quarters.[131] Nine of the men were found sleeping in the attic, and eight were found sleeping in the garage. No formal action was taken against the homeowner, but he was warned to reduce the number of tenants in the home. Other camp operators in the area were also warned that more inspections were to follow, and similar violations at multi-occupancy dwellings would be strictly enforced.

THE MIGRATORY LABOR SYSTEM

THE CREW LEADERS

Identifying many of the labor camps that once dominated the eastern end of Long Island is only part of the story. To fully understand this history, a close review of how the labor camps operated is also required. This section explores the pivotal role of the crew leaders, the recruitment process and the economic exploitation of migrant farmworkers that was at the heart of Suffolk County's migratory labor system.

The 1960 documentary *Harvest of Shame* first exposed the treatment of migrant workers throughout this country. The film opens in the small town of Belle Glade, Florida, where a group of farm labor contractors, called "hawkers," announced the going pay rate to a crowd of laborers who were desperate for work. One grower who was familiar with the process stated, "We used to own our slaves. Now we just rent them."

The recruitment process of migrant laborers has been described as a remnant of the padrone system; a system of contract labor used to secure immigrant laborers who sought work in the United States. The roots of the padrone system date back to Italy's unification in 1861, which caused a consolidation of land and led to a loss of jobs, forcing many people to leave the country in search of work.[132] A padrone, which is an Italian word loosely translated into English as "boss" or "manager," was essentially a labor broker who contracted with employers to fill a labor shortage with skilled and unskilled workers. Padrones also arranged the transportation and housing for the workers they recruited. Since most of the immigrant workers lacked the funds to pay for these items, the fees were placed on credit and were later deducted from their earnings. Since it is so rife with abuse and manipulation, this system has been widely criticized as a form of human trafficking.

The migratory labor system practiced on eastern Long Island throughout the twentieth century was akin to the padrone system. Crew leaders (sometimes referred to as crew chiefs) contracted with Long Island growers to supply the much-needed labor for their harvests. In exchange, they were paid a fixed amount of money by the growers for each day of work performed by one of his or her recruits. Crew leaders also leased the labor camps from the growers to house the migrant workers at overpriced rental rates that were deducted from their weekly earnings. Lastly, crew leaders retained full control of the pay and care for the workers at the labor camps.[133]

In larger camps, like the one in Cutchogue, camp managers were also used and, although they exercised authority over the workers, their role was largely relegated to managing the facility. Once a crew leader developed a business relationship with a group of growers, he or she would quite often continue to do business with them year after year. By design, this contractual arrangement gave the crew leaders unfettered control for everything from camp operations to the pay and care of the migrant workers. In turn, the growers were free to use the benefit of having a pool of laborers on hand without any responsibility for them or their living conditions.

Once a contract was established, the next step in the process was to secure a group of farm laborers. Crew leaders, who were usually Black southern men, visited economically depressed U.S. states, such as Alabama, Arkansas, the Carolinas, Florida and Virginia, to recruit impoverished Black laborers with promises of fair wages and adequate housing. Others were known to visit bars, soup kitchens and homeless shelters in various East Coast cities, seeking vulnerable men to perform farm labor. Crew leaders also provided for the transportation for the workers to New York and back to their home states at the end of the harvest season. All items from transportation, lodging, meals and beverages were charged to the workers on credit, typically at overinflated prices, and the payment was deducted from their weekly earnings.

Such power did not come without some lawful oversight. In New York, crew leaders were required to be licensed by the Department of Labor to recruit and employ migrant laborers, and growers could not hire crew leaders who were unlicensed. Prospective crew leaders could be denied a license if they had been convicted within five years of various felonies.[134] However, crew leaders with criminal records could escape this restriction by having their spouses apply for the license, and they would then assume the duties. Crew leaders were also responsible for maintaining employment and payroll records, which were often poorly maintained or completely fraudulent, and maintaining the labor camp in accordance with state law.

Crew leaders were a foundational part of the migratory labor system in Suffolk County. They were sanctioned by the state to serve as labor contractors. The migrant workers were housed at labor camps owned by the growers who were able to outsource all responsibility for them to the crew leaders while reaping the benefits of the pool of laborers housed nearby. With authority akin to a viceroy, the crew leaders recruited migrant farmworkers and transported them back to Long Island, where they assumed full control over the pay, working conditions and the very lives of the workers, who were most often left irrevocably mired in debt. This was the migratory labor system practiced on Long Island during the twentieth century. The next section will detail how deeply flawed and rife with profound abuse and corruption this system truly was.

Labor Camp Economics

"Dust for Blood"

From the very inception of the labor camp era, widespread complaints of corruption and abuse were filed, which compelled state officials to investigate. In 1961, a subcommittee led by U.S. representative from New York Herbert Zelenko, was formed to investigate a series of allegations of abuse at migrant labor camps throughout New York and New Jersey.[135] Despite facing threats of witness intimidation, a fifty-two-year-old migrant woman named Betty Jean Johnson testified before the committee and stated, "They bring us up from the South and make slaves out of us." She testified that a crew leader named Carl Beamon brought her from Virginia to Long Island and told her that she would earn $1.25 per hour. Instead, she worked long hours and earned only between $3.00 and $5.00 per week after deductions for rent, meals and other fees. Mrs. Johnson added that Social Security was deducted from her pay, even though she did not have a Social Security number. Another witness, Rebecca Poe, testified that she worked six days per week, earning $1.00 per hour, and her pay only averaged about $7.00 to $8.00 per week. When she complained at the city hall in Riverhead, she was told that there was nothing that could be done.[136]

Despite the allegations and ensuing investigations, the inner workings of the migratory labor system remained relatively unknown to lawmakers and the general public. That all changed with the 1968 release of the documentary *What Harvest for the Reaper?*, a film that provides a vivid account of the economic exploitation of migrant farmworkers at the Cutchogue labor camp.[137] The film begins in the impoverished town of Forest City, Arkansas, where Andrew Anderson, a crew leader who contracted with the Eastern Suffolk Cooperative to provide laborers, began recruiting young men to work on the farms of Long Island. Anderson lured the workers, all of whom were Black men, with promises of good wages, steady work, decent housing and the comfort of a "centrally located restaurant" on the grounds, which was owned and operated by Anderson and his wife. Pursuant to his contract with the farmers, Anderson was paid sixty cents per worker for each day that they worked and an additional twenty-five cents per hour for each of the laborers who worked in potato processing plant and nurseries.

The next day, six men joined Anderson on his bus for the 1,200-mile trek to Long Island. The charge for the round-trip bus ride was thirty dollars per man. Since none of them could afford to pay the transportation costs, they immediately became indebted to Anderson. When the bus arrived at the Cutchogue labor camp, the men were assigned their sleeping quarters. One man, Charlie White, was assigned a small, grimy room littered with debris and holes in the walls, and even though a fire at the camp in 1961 killed four people, White's room was not fireproofed.

In the morning, the workers gathered at the Dixie Belle Tavern, the centrally located restaurant that Anderson spoke of when he recruited them. Breakfast meals typically included a small amount of sausage, rice and "an occasional egg," which cost an average of eighty-five cents, made payable directly to Mr. Anderson. At the time, a state law limited the costs of food to sixteen dollars per week per person. However, crew leaders like Andrew Anderson found a way to beat the system by selling food without any beverages and then by selling eight-cent cans of soda for twenty-five cents or thirty-five cents if purchased on credit. Since the majority of the workers did not have cash on hand, all charges were placed on credit to be deducted, along with other expenses, directly from their weekly paychecks.

Pints of a cheap local wine were regularly sold at the camp for $1.00 or $1.25. The same sized bottle cost $0.51 at liquor stores in town; however, since Anderson was known to retaliate against anyone who purchased liquor outside of the camp, the workers typically resorted to paying the overinflated prices.

After breakfast, most workers boarded the bus and were taken to nearby farms for the day. The cost for the round trip was $1.25, again payable to Mr. Anderson. Trips to further locations, such as Riverhead, cost as much as $3.00, but those rides were strictly subject to his whims. Those workers who fell out of favor with Anderson were left behind without earning an income while still incurring the daily debt of residing at the camp. Some growers, like William Chudiak, who was also the president of the Eastern Suffolk Cooperative at the time, arrived at the camp to pick up a small group of workers. The men jumped onto the back of his pickup truck and were driven to work on his farm. At another farm, some of the men discovered that a group of workers at a nearby plant nursery were performing the same work and earned $1.75 per hour, while they earned $1.35 per hour. They resented being paid much less for the same work but ultimately kept their complaints hidden from Anderson for fear of reprisal.

At the time this film was made, strawberries were ranked as the third most productive crop on Long Island and were harvested from June to August. A group of six migrant workers were filmed picking strawberries at the going rate of $0.10 per quart picked. Together, the six men earned $2.00 each for six hours of work for a total of $12.00, while at a nearby auction, all of the strawberries picked on that day yielded close to $200.00. Later, the film depicts several tourists who, for a small fee, were able to pick strawberries for themselves. The contrast between a farmworker who toiled in the field picking strawberries for survival and a tourist who picked them for leisure could not be starker.

On another day, Charlie White and several other workers were driven to a nearby farm to pick string beans. They began the day at 6:00 a.m., worked until noon and were paid $1.00 per hamper of string beans picked. Charlie White worked for six hours, picked two hampers of string beans and earned $2.00. However, since Andrew Anderson collected $0.15 on each dollar they earned, which was among the many various fees that he charged to his workers, White was paid $1.70 for his work.

As was the case with all crew leaders, Anderson strictly controlled the hourly pay for each worker and the number of hours they would work. When equipment malfunctioned or if there were other work stoppages that were not the fault of their own, the workers were unpaid during that time. This is critical because it drastically reduced the hourly pay they were supposed to have earned for that workday. For instance, at the minimum wage rate of $1.35 per hour for an eight-hour day, a farmworker would earn $10.80 for the day. However, if there was a breakdown in machinery that took four hours to repair, that same worker was forced to wait until work resumed and would be paid for only four hours of the eight-hour day. Thus his hourly rate would be cut in half and he would earn $5.40 for the same eight-hour period, all while he continued to accrue his daily expenses.

Charlie White and another migrant worker were asked to share their income and expenses. They each explained that in one week, they were charged five dollars for rent, eighteen to nineteen dollars for food and drink, a blanket fee of five dollars and a fuel charge of two dollars, along with other incremental costs, which they could not explain, for a total of approximately forty dollars. Even if Anderson's calculations were trustworthy, an assumption that strained credulity, their average total earnings for the workweek were forty-seven dollars, which, after deducting their expenses, left them very little money each week. The grim reality was that most migrant farmworkers barely broke even or consistently owed more money than they earned. By the end of the season, some were fortunate enough to afford the transportation costs to return home, but most remained indebted to the crew leader well into the next harvest season.

Payday for the migrant workers was typically on Saturdays. One farmworker grimly described it as "dust for blood." At the Cutchogue camp, all of the wages and expenses were based exclusively on Anderson's bookkeeping. As was the case with most crew leaders, migrant workers were required to sign a form acknowledging receipt of their earnings. Once their pay was received, there was no recourse or ability for the migrant workers to dispute the calculations. Threats of physical violence or other forms of retribution rendered it more expedient to remain silent or suffer the dire consequences.

Anderson typically demanded that the workers cash their checks with him. Those who would dare to venture to a nearby bank to cash their check had limited time to do so because of the late hours the checks were distributed, and if they did, they were likely to suffer the consequences. Of Anderson, one worker stated, "We do all the work, and he gets paid." Another worker, who was just fourteen years old, complained that he had been trying to leave the camp for months but had been unable to save up enough money to do so. He added, "You ain't never getting out of debt with Anderson. You in debt when you started, you in debt when you leave."

Some crew leaders paid their workers in cash. One migrant worker, Otis Johnson, explained the process, stating, "They give you the envelope. Before you open it, you have to sign it. On the envelope there might be $60, $200, $300, but in the envelope, was a slip of what you owed him out of payment for wine, sleeping, eating....On the outside of the envelope it says you made $80 this week; inside the envelope is $5." When asked what would happen if a man complained about his pay, he replied, "He gets his ass kicked."[138] Phillip Borrero, assistant director of the Suffolk County Migratory Affairs Council, stated, "Many migrants die under mysterious circumstances and we make investigations into these untimely deaths. Foul play is suspected quite often but the allegations cannot be proven, and the medical examiner's office is kept busy."[139]

Clearly, this system favored the crew leaders, and many of them prospered greatly. Reverend Arthur Bryant explained that Andrew Anderson was one of the more sophisticated crew leaders who made a lucrative living, which he estimated to be nearly $40,000.00 per year. Bryant explained that Anderson knew that the minimum wage in Arkansas at the time was $1.00 per hour, but workers there were exploited and probably earned closer to $0.40 per hour. With this knowledge, Anderson convinced them that they could earn up to $1.35 or more per hour on Long Island, and they were naturally inclined to accept the terms. However, from the moment the farmworkers stepped onto the bus and for their entire stay on Long Island, they were at the complete mercy of Andrew Anderson.

By its very nature, the crew leader system was rife with abuse and manipulation that left thousands of migrant farmworkers mired in irrevocable debt. Reverend Arthur Bryant stated, "Migrants caught up in the stream are powerless and voteless because they are homeless. They are also powerless economically because they are deprived the right of collective bargaining. And because they are powerless economically, they frequently become powerless to break away and enter into the mainstream of American life. They are serfs subject to the will of the owner and even the finest paternalistic measures accomplish nothing to remove the chains of slavery." Bryant compared the plight of the migrants to the exploited crewmen in the nineteenth-century whaling industry and added, "False promises and Shanghai methods are still used to induce men into a life of death, hardship and hopelessness."[140]

While the documentary *What Harvest for the Reaper?* focused on Andrew Anderson, there were many other crew leaders who operated similarly or even worse. Mr. Borrero railed against the exploitation of the migrant workers by the crew leaders. He stated, "A recent case in question involved a crew chief who went to Alabama to recruit migrants in a van. He promised the unemployed workers that they would be paid $150 a week to work on Long Island. After working for a week, the pay was no way near what they were promised, and the crew chief threatened them with bodily harm and the fact that he was the authority so far as they were concerned."[141]

There have been a few, albeit limited, cases where crew leaders were subjected to criminal prosecution. In 1972, James L. Brown was charged with cheating seven migrant workers at the H. Sacks & Sons Potato processing plant in Mattituck of their pay for a total of $389.[142] Brown was also charged with failing to obtain a state license to become a crew leader, which came with a maximum fine of $10,000 and imprisonment for up to one year. The case was successfully prosecuted with the assistance of a volunteer group called Long Island Volunteers. Mr. Brown pleaded guilty to reduced charges and agreed to pay all of the money back to the workers. As part of his plea deal, Brown was banned from working as a crew leader for up to one year. At the conclusion of the trial, Mary Chase Stone, founder of Long Island Volunteers, stated, "We've broken our backs for seven years trying to find a group of people who would stand up there [in court]. It shows that migrants can take their grievances to court just like anybody else."

Several other crew leaders were prosecuted for various crimes, including acts of violence.[143] In 1972, a crew leader named James Covil at the H. Sacks & Sons labor camp on Osborne Avenue in Riverhead was charged with two counts of second-degree assault after a dispute erupted with two migrant workers about their pay. Covil beat one man with a hammer and shattered the jaw of another with his fists.[144] Later, a crew leader at the at the Cutchogue labor camp, Ernest Mitchell, was charged with beating a migrant woman named Blanche Davenport with a broom, a hammer and his fists. He also forced another worker to walk barefoot for two miles and stole wages from another. Despite these successful prosecutions, justice for migrant farmworkers was rarely achieved, and manipulative crew leaders were able to profit for many years in this vicious cycle of exploitation.

The heart of the corruption in the migratory labor system was unquestionably evident in the role played by the crew leaders who ruthlessly exerted economic, societal, physical and psychological dominance over the migrant farmworkers at the labor camps. Much of this abuse would have remained largely hidden from the public without the documentary *What Harvest for the Reaper?* The film is a priceless revelation of the exploitative nature of the migratory labor system of Suffolk County.

THE ODYSSEY OF ALFONZO MAHONE

Few examples can more accurately capture the abuse suffered by migrant workers at the hands of crew leaders than the story of Alfonzo Mahone, who as a young Black teenager found himself far from his home near Macon, Georgia, and working in two Long Island labor camps. Mahone, who was fifteen years old at the time, was subjected to the manipulation and abuse typically found in the migratory labor system of Suffolk County.[145]

Mahone's odyssey began in July 1968. His mother struggled to make ends meet as she raised the family of seven by herself. One day, while he was visiting some of his friends, a small white school bus stopped and one of his friends exited to ask Mahone if he wanted to join him to work on a farm in Virginia to pick apples. A tall Black woman named Miss Viola exited a car that accompanied the bus and explained that they were recruiting farm laborers and, if her son wanted work, he would receive fair pay, along with food and a place to rest. She also promised to be "responsible" for his well-being. With few economic prospects available, Mahone's mother reluctantly agreed to let her son join the group of workers.

That evening, the passengers were forced to sleep on the bus and did so every night for a week. The good food that was promised consisted of a few slices of bologna, pork and beans and peanut butter and jelly sandwiches. When they entered Virginia, they met with a crew leader named Goldie who offered them work picking tomatoes for sixty to seventy dollars a week. "He gave us a dollar each and bought cigarettes for some of the others," said Mahone, who, along with eight others from the bus, agreed to leave with Goldie. They worked for a week and, after deductions were made for food and other costs, were paid a meager fourteen dollars.

According to Mahone, picking tomatoes was backbreaking work, and Goldie was overly harsh with them, which caused him to search for other work opportunities. He met another man, Charles Wright, who offered to pay off his debt and find him better work in New York. Wright told Mahone that he was a crew leader registered in Riverhead, even though records would later reveal that his license had expired one year earlier, and he joined five other workers in Wright's white Cadillac for the long ride to Long Island.

Mahone worked for a week at the Pollack labor camp in Bridgehampton and was paid ten dollars. A short while later, he began working at a nearby potato grading shed owned by the Southampton Produce Company, which was adorned with a sign that read "A bruised potato never heals." The work was grimy and grueling, and after many relentless hours, Mahone slept in a filthy labor camp with twenty other workers near the back of a small house.

A short time later, Mahone sustained an injury to his hand, and he refused to continue working. An unsympathetic foreman at the shed barked, "You get your small ass out of here and get back to the camp." He left the plant and was walking along Montauk Highway when Charles Wright drove up and shouted some obscenities at him before evicting him from the camp, leaving him stranded. Mahone hitchhiked to Riverhead and spent a few nights in the care of the nonprofit group Long Island Volunteers, which eventually secured his safe return home to Georgia.

During a span of one week at Southampton Produce plant, Mahone earned a total of $40.80, at the rate of $1.70 per hour, but $18.40 was deducted from his pay for room and board. Later on, the state labor department was able to recoup the $22.40 he earned but was never paid. The labor department also recouped $33.80 for his work at the Pollack labor camp. Moreover, both camps were cited for having unlawfully used child labor and for failing to pay wages and acting as a labor contractor without a license. Sadly, these situations were not uncommon. Reverend Arthur Bryant described it: "The quick pickups for work, the promise of wages, the promise that a packing camp has everything, all the false promises. It sounds like the way they used to pick up kids for the circus."

In some ways, the story of Alfonzo Mahone ended much better than it did for most other migrant workers of the time. He was able to recoup his hard-earned wages and was fortunate to leave the migrant stream and return home safely. However, he was a fifteen-year-old boy who was lured to work by lies, subjected to economic manipulation and cruelty, forced to sleep in poor living conditions, denied medical treatment for an injury he sustained, deprived of the timely payment of his hard-earned wages and abandoned to find his own way home. Such an odyssey should never be forgotten, as it serves as a stark reminder of the plight of all migrant farmworkers.

THE PUERTO RICAN LABOR CONTRACTS

The Suffolk County migratory labor system was notorious for the exploitation of farmworkers whose terms and conditions of employment, including living expenses, were left entirely to the whim of unscrupulous crew leaders and indifferent growers. However, there was a notable exception for a small group of contract laborers from Puerto Rico, and the improved working conditions for these workers could not have been clearer.

By the middle of the twentieth century, Puerto Rico expressed serious concerns for laborers who left the island to work in mainland United States. The Puerto Rican Department of Labor showed newsreels that warned laborers of the adverse conditions that generally awaited them in New York and other places.[146] The film's narrator warned, "One runs grave risks to health. The housing situation is acute. Rents are high. It is difficult to find a place to live. Unemployment is serious for those who do not speak English. All this creates a difficult social situation." This dire concern led the Puerto Rican government to establish labor contracts for workers who left the island to work in various states, including New York.

In 1948, the Puerto Rican Department of Labor established the migration division. This agency was formed to create labor contracts and transport farmworkers to eastern states.[147] On July 8, 1948, the first group of Puerto Rican farmworkers arrived on a DC-3 plane at MacArthur Airport to work on Long Island. By the early 1960s, hundreds of Puerto Rican farmworkers were hired to work on farms throughout New York and New Jersey, with approximately two hundred workers hired to work on eastern Long Island. Many of these workers were employed through labor contracts that guaranteed a wide array of terms and conditions of employment.

Much of the success of the Puerto Rican labor contracts can be attributed to the efforts of Alan Perl, a labor lawyer from New York retained by the Puerto Rican Department of Labor to negotiate contracts with farm associations that sought to employ Puerto Rican agricultural workers. These labor contracts required growers to pay a prevailing wage rate to farmworkers and provide a guarantee of no less than 160 hours of work every four weeks, whether or not they worked the full 160 hours.[148] Thus when machines were shut down at no fault of their own, the employees were paid their hourly pay while awaiting repairs. Moreover, growers who employed Puerto Rican contract workers were required to provide for their transportation to and from the farms, and food was often provided for them in the field, in a soup-kitchen manner, all at no cost to the workers. The labor camps were also required to provide access to workers' compensation benefits if they suffered a work-related injury.

Workers under these contracts were able to make demands for improvements, and, although workplace discipline could be issued, no grower could unilaterally fire any of the workers without the consent of the other growers in the respective association. This extraordinary level of

Left: Farmworkers from Puerto Rico disembarking from an airplane in Buffalo, New York, in 1948. *Courtesy of the Records of the Migration Division, Archives of the Puerto Rican Diaspora, Centro de Estudios Puertorriquenos, Hunter College, City University of New York.*

Opposite: A chartered flight with migrant farmworkers from Puerto Rico in 1948. *Courtesy of the Records of the Migration Division, Archives of the Puerto Rican Diaspora, Centro de Estudios Puertorriquenos, Hunter College, City University of New York.*

job security was not available to any other migrant farmworker at the time. The Jamaican workers had similar contracts with various farm associations. However, workers under those contracts who did not perform satisfactory work could be sent back to Jamaica at their own expense. This, according to Mr. Perl, created a far more "docile" group of workers when compared to the Puerto Rican workers, who were keenly aware of their rights.

Puerto Rican contract workers also received health coverage, which was partially funded by the workers, with most of the costs paid by the farm associations. In some cases, large farm associations in Connecticut and New Jersey paid the full cost of health care that was administered at medical facilities near the farms. While no records could be found detailing this level of access to healthcare for workers on Long Island, clearly, a model for such benefits existed for many of them.

Lastly, the growers who refused to abide by the contract were pressured by other association members to comply or risk expulsion from the group.

Moreover, while these contracts did not include specific sanitary codes for housing or meals, they did have language that called for "adequate and sanitary housing accommodations." While this was indeed broad contract language, Mr. Perl explained that, as the drafter of the contracts, he was most often the one who did the interpreting and usually in the favor of the workers.

There can be no doubt that the working conditions for the Puerto Rican contract laborers were vastly superior to the overwhelming majority of workers who languished without a labor contract. Reverend Arthur Bryant stated, "I would say that Puerto Ricans, under the contract's protection do fare better than the continental workers because the commonwealth has the contract as a model."[149]

Unfortunately, labor contracts that provided prevailing wages, guaranteed hours, health care and other benefits for migrant farmworkers were not a favored model among the growers in Suffolk County, and those who were fortunate enough to have a contract were in the vast minority. According to a joint survey compiled by the United States Employment Service and the Suffolk County Department of Health, out of the 4,950 farmworkers in Suffolk County in 1954, only 309 of them were contract Puerto Rican farmworkers. By 1960, that number declined to 195 Puerto Rican farmworkers.[150] Most assuredly, the growers on Long Island viewed these contracts as too costly, which ultimately led them to use non-contract farmworkers instead. Without any contractual rights, these migrant workers languished in labor camps that worsened with each passing year.

5

THE TOLL ON THE LIFE
OF A MIGRANT WORKER

Psychological Effects

The Suffolk County migratory labor system was a complex blend of economic and industrial factors intertwined with labor and immigration laws. However, above all else, this is a human story that requires a review of the emotional and physical suffering faced by those trapped in this system. This section delves into the toll on the life of a migrant worker.

In the 1968 documentary *What Harvest for the Reaper?* the narrator candidly states, "Early in the season, Cutchogue was a vacation resort, one of the prides of Long Island's North Fork. The prim town is resplendent with schools, churches and old homes. It also has a migrant labor camp." With foreboding music, the scene cuts to a close-up of barbed wire spanning across the perimeter of the Cutchogue labor camp, with the Dixie Belle Inn restaurant shown in the background. In a fire at the Jacobs labor camp in Bridgehampton, the bodies of three migrant workers were found trapped in a room with a door that had been nailed shut. Lifelong Greenport resident Josephine Watkins-Johnson recalled an instance when two migrant workers fled a labor camp and made it to the nearby train, only to be hauled off, beaten and forced back to the camp. Carl Beamon had once locked a migrant worker inside his labor camp and forced him to tend to his sick wife, and there were reports of men and women being taken against their will and forced to work on Long Island farms, a term that became known as being "shanghaied." While these occurrences conjure up the belief that the labor camps were prisons where migrant workers were held in literal bondage, they were relatively rare and had extenuating circumstances. Ultimately, there is no specific evidence to support the notion that the labor camps were prisons. To the contrary, migrant workers were generally free to come and go as they wished. However, this history will show that there was more than one way for a person to be imprisoned.

Migrant laborers worked long, grueling hours picking everything from strawberries to potatoes on Long Island farms from March through November. Since the labor camps were situated miles away from the nearest towns, and the workers typically had no mode of transportation, visiting a town to enjoy a semblance of normal day life was not a viable option. As a result, migrant workers were generally relegated to the confines of the labor camps.[151] One reporter wrote, "Good or bad, nearly all of the camps are situated away from the main roads, isolated from the farmsteads and rural communities. Neither the camps nor the migrants come often into the awareness of the society with which they exist."[152]

When the weather was bad or if they were excluded from performing work by a punitive crew leader, the workers remained at the camp with nothing to do while incurring their daily debt. Local reporter Ruth Schier once wrote, "We forget that when the working week is over, or when the rain pours down, or the crops are slow to ripen, there is nothing but empty time for the migrant. He has nothing to do, nowhere to go and usually no way to get there."[153] Not all workers remained idle during periods of no work. At the Cutchogue labor camp, a group of Puerto Rican workers who were once recruited to pick strawberries understood the costs they incurred each day at the camp, so during poor weather, they ventured into the nearby woods to club rabbits and to the Long Island Sound to dig for clams.[154] However, this was a rare and limited example of workers engaging in self sustenance during periods of no work.

At the camps, entertainment was a rare luxury. Some had jukeboxes and others had television sets, but these devices were usually broken. Nearly all of the camps had no telephones. Thus the life of the migrant farmworker was replete with boredom and isolation, which essentially made them prisoners of the labor camp. On Christmas Day in 1969, local reporter George DeWan visited the Zahler labor camp in Aquebogue. He summarized his experience as follows: "In the camp there was also a television set, but it was broken. The room was dark and quiet as the men generally moped around, looking bored. Thomas Benthall, 56, a North Carolinian man who said he never smoked or drank, sat on the top of his bunk bed with his feet hanging over the side, and he just stared off into space."

The bullpen-style sleeping quarters at the camps allowed no personal space for workers to relax peacefully in bed or maintain any type of privacy. Since there was no furniture, the workers were unable to secure any meager belongings they might have had. Those with personal items of value became frequent targets of thieves or bullies at the camp who often stole such property or simply took it by force. Without adequate and private living space, the migrant workers were denied the sanctity of all human beings. "I think the housing in itself degrades the man and dehumanizes him and finally renders him completely helpless to fight about anything," stated Reverend Bryant.[155]

The feeling of helplessness from the economic manipulation and abuse at the hands of ruthless and corrupt crew leaders only compounded the abysmal life of migrant workers at the camps. Since they were denied the right to union representation and were not citizens of the state, migrant workers were unable to make any changes to these conditions. Reverend Bryant discussed the adverse impacts such exploitation had on the migrant workers, stating, "He releases his anger in an acceptable way when he leads the camp in the singing of old prison songs. Sometimes he gets it out of his system by ordering weaker men around. He is angry because he has no way to force the crew leader to pay him a wage other men in the camp receive."[156] Moreover, since the camps affected the community in a negative way, there was little sympathy from the public to help. In *What Harvest for the Reaper?* the psyche of the migrant workers is characterized as "the humiliation, the being without, is to the worker the natural air he breathes every day."

The migrant workers were steeped in boredom and isolation, denied the privacy and comfort that all human beings should enjoy and victimized by chronic exploitation. In this punishing environment, many of them turned to alcohol to cope with their despair. To further their exploitative grip, camp owners applied for licenses to lawfully sell liquor at the camps. As early as 1952, the Eastern Suffolk Cooperative obtained a beverage license, which allowed for the sale of liquor at the Cutchogue labor camp.[157] Other camps simply allowed access to illegal liquor dealers to prey on the migrant workers. The destructive force of alcohol abuse left the workers foggy and more dependent each day, which served as another measure of control over the workforce. Andrew Anderson, the crew leader at the Cutchogue camp, once stated, "A man who can't read and is drunk on wine every night doesn't even know how to complain."[158]

In July 1970, *Newsday* reporter Les Payne spent one week undercover at a labor camp on Old Quogue Road in Riverhead.[159] Drawing on his experience as young boy who picked cotton in the fields of Alabama, Payne disguised himself as a migrant worker named Bubba to blend in with the other camp workers. Payne's firsthand account vividly describes the abysmal life of a farmworker in a migrant labor camp—one mired in boredom, dependency, exploitation and violence. He opened his reporting stating, "It was 6:45 am Friday, the day before the Fourth of July, the day that 'the eagle flies.' Payday: the climax of the migrant laborers' week. I had waited for the day for what seemed like a month. The other days had all been self-contained, each with its own strange beauty, each with its special heartbreak."

Wine was the most favored drink at labor camps. Payne described it as "the lifeblood of the migrant worker." He further explained how the crew leader, named Brown, used wine as a vehicle to control the emotions of the workers. "We turned to wine out of despair, loneliness, pain, and depression brought on by boredom and the alienated lifestyle," explained Payne. "By controlling the flow of wine, the crew chief controlled our very lives. He dished it out at morning, noon, and night, on credit and at exaggerated prices. When the men got restless and asked for pay, the crew chief gave them wine."

Byran Hamlin, who served as the president of the board of directors of the Bridgehampton Child Care Center, believed that crew leaders purposefully recruited alcoholics because "they are easier to control and they can usually be paid in cheap wine."[160] Carl Beamon was known to scour bars, soup kitchens and homeless shelters throughout many East Coast cities with his long-time acquaintance William "Big Willy" Moore to forcefully recruit vulnerable transients for farm labor.

Twister, a cheap and highly addictive California grape wine with an artificial mint flavor that had 20 percent alcohol, was readily available at the camps. At the time of Payne's report, the price for a bottle at a nearby store was $0.64. However, Brown distributed bottles on credit for a fee of $1.50 per bottle. Such markups were common in most of the camps, and workers were often charged whether they drank the wine or not. "It is costly for the migrant," stated reporter Ruth Schier, "but life is so aimless, any kind of fun is better than no fun at all."

During his testimony before Congress, Reverend Arthur Bryant spoke about the destructive forces that surrounded the migrant workers. He stated, "But this man has driven his rage down deep, repressed and hidden it where it can't escape. His rage is turned against himself because he is powerless to stand up to his crew leader, powerless to stand up to his fellow workers, powerless to change his life." When the migrants turn to alcohol, Bryant stated, "He no longer has a choice. He must commit suicide slowly or quickly. He hates the powerlessness within himself. He hates himself. His dream of a better world will not be in this world."

For most migrant workers, farm labor was all they had ever known. Thus the prospect of a better future was typically dim. This was particularly the case for those without family or those who left family behind to work on Long Island. Sister Maureen Duffy of the Nursing Sisters of the Sick Poor, who provided medical treatment and counseling services to migrant workers in Bridgehampton, stated, "The main problem is the total absence of family life. They are constant job seekers on a path of rootlessness. Without the encouragement of a family, there's a complete lack of security and feeling of belonging. They're never sure how long a job will last or even of the camp they'll be assigned to. This is the worst kind of poverty."[161]

Children of migrant workers faced the greatest threat to their future prospects. In *Harvest of Shame*, Edward R. Murrow interviews impoverished families whose children were forced to forsake school so that they could tend to their younger siblings while their parents worked long days in the fields. A nine-year-old boy named Jerome was interviewed as he sat on a bed in a rat-infested room of a labor camp in Florida looking after his younger siblings while his mother worked ten-hour days on a nearby farm. Since she earned $1.00 per day and the cost of meals was $2.00 and day care was $0.85, Jerome's mother had no choice but to leave the younger siblings in his care, which left him unable to attend school.

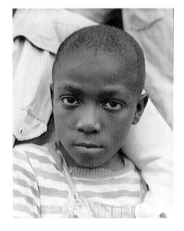

Jerome's fate was common among nearly all of the children of migrant workers. According to statistics at the time the film was made, children of migrant workers had the highest rate of illiteracy in the country, where one in five hundred children finished grade school, one in five thousand finished high school and there was no record of any child of a migrant worker earning a college degree. In New York, the only known school

A child of a migrant worker in Bridgeton, New Jersey, 1942. Many children either worked on the farms with their parents or stayed at the labor camps to look after their siblings. This denied them the opportunity to have a proper education. *Courtesy of the Library of Congress.*

for migrant children was at the Cutchogue labor camp. However, Helen Wright Prince explained that conditions at the camp school were not optimal for learning. In this punishing environment, children were left to fend for themselves, and the denial of an education would doom a whole generation to a life of exploitation, forever searching for menial work with little hope of a better future.

The migrant farmworkers who inhabited labor camps were subjected to an abundance of isolation, degradation, dependency and exploitation, all of which took a heavy psychological toll on their lives. Despite the grim conditions, most of them were driven by poverty to return year after year with full knowledge of what awaited them. As a result, many migrant workers resorted to alcohol to suppress their rage and sorrow, and camp operators were more than eager to oblige because it served as an effective way to control the workforce. While the migrant farmworkers in Suffolk County were not held in literal bondage, the psychological effects they faced at the labor camps were virtually synonymous with a prison-like atmosphere, the escape of which was rarely accomplished.

HEALTH AND SAFETY CONCERNS

The life of a migratory labor system was fraught with physical dangers. According to 1971 statistics from the U.S. Senate Subcommittee on Migratory Labor, the life expectancy for the average migrant worker was forty-nine years old, and the infant mortality rate was 125 times higher than the national average.[162] Malnutrition and poor diet were all too common. A nationwide survey conducted in 1975 showed that the children of migrant workers suffered from widespread stomach and intestinal illnesses, with symptoms ranging from diarrhea to dehydration.[163] Maintaining proper hygiene was always difficult at unsanitary labor camps, which often caused a variety of skin infections, including ringworm.

Farmworkers also suffered from a variety of illnesses related to contact with pesticides. Before it was banned by the federal government in 1972, Dichlorodiphenyltrichloroethane, commonly known as DDT, was a widely used pesticide. It was later proven to be very harmful to humans and wildlife. DDT was replaced with organophosphate pesticides, which were also deadly poisons. Since these workers had daily contact with these chemicals and had little or no access to medical treatment, they were susceptible to pesticide poisoning, with symptoms that included nausea, dizziness, diarrhea and blurred vision. Since instances of pesticide poisoning were not properly recorded, it might never be known if a health crisis of this nature existed.[164]

Migrant workers were also vulnerable to weather-related illnesses, such as heat stroke and fatigue. During the colder seasons, they were vulnerable to bronchial illnesses and similar maladies. At the Cutchogue labor camp, several migrant workers once complained of being sick and refused to work. This angered crew leader Isiah Moore, who was deprived of the sixty cents per man that he would have been paid if they worked that day. In retaliation, Moore disconnected the fuel line to the kerosene heater, forcing the men to huddle close together for warmth. Within two weeks, three of the men died of pneumonia.[165]

Many farmworkers suffered from a variety of maladies, including mental illness, sexually transmitted diseases and alcohol abuse. The spread of infectious diseases in unsanitary and crowded labor camps was also a grave concern. Nationally, in 1960, the death rate of migrant farmworkers by tuberculosis alone was double the rate of most other American workers.[166] A decade later, rates of flu, tuberculosis, pneumonia and other respiratory conditions were 200 percent higher than the national average. In 1980, 104 of 392 migrant workers at various Long Island labor camps tested positive for tuberculosis.[167]

Little or no access to proper healthcare often had deadly consequences. On April 8, 1956, the lifeless body of Arthur Drew was found in a snowstorm off Route 25 near Mattituck. Drew, who was a migrant worker, was reported to have lived alone in a shack off Legion Avenue. Despite the frigid weather, he was found wearing only light clothing. An autopsy concluded that Drew suffered from subacute bronchial pneumonia resulting from tuberculosis of the lungs.[168]

On December 22, 1965, the body of migrant farmworker Willie Jeff Lawrence was found outside of his shanty home off Oregon Road in Mattituck. Another migrant worker, Toby Armstrong, who was living with Lawrence, told police that an unidentified man had broken into their home one week earlier and attacked them both. As a result, Lawrence suffered from concussion-like symptoms until his death a few days later. An autopsy concluded that the cause of death was a fractured skull.[169]

During the morning hours of April 7, 1969, the lifeless body of a migrant laborer named James Bittle was found at the Lipco-Agway labor camp on Edgar Avenue in Aquebogue.[170] The evening before his death, Bittle had complained of pains, fever and nausea and was treated at Central Suffolk

Hospital before being released. Local police investigated his death and found no signs of criminality. The Suffolk County Human Rights Commission openly questioned why Mr. Bittle, who appeared to be critically ill, was not admitted to the hospital. James Brown, the camp's crew chief, stated, "I've tried to get all my men into the hospital at some time. They'll give them a pill, but they won't take them in."

Lastly, in December 1971, a migrant worker named Pedro Fuentes suffered an epileptic seizure while walking in the woods between labor camps.[171] His lifeless body was found frozen behind a rotted tree days later. These four tragedies stemmed from illness or injury that might have been preventable if these workers had proper access to health care.

Farm labor is generally undesirable. The repetitive daylong performance of walking, crawling, stooping and kneeling is incredibly taxing on the body and leaves farmworkers prone to many injuries.[172] By 1970, the national accident rate for farmworkers was three times as great as that of any other occupation.[173] Many injuries were caused by the stress of having to harvest crops quickly. "It's the hurry, the fatigue, the taking shortcuts to beat the rain," explained Don DiBillo, the director of member services for Farm Family Insurance Company.[174] The risk of injury was greatly compounded by stingy farmers who stubbornly refused to invest in new equipment. "Half the equipment I've used should be in a junkyard," explained one migrant worker. "You know you're taking a chance, but you've got to get on it if you want to make a living."[175]

Prior to 1965, migrant farmworkers were excluded from benefits under the New York Workman's Compensation Act.[176] During that time, if a worker suffered a work-related injury, the only recourse was to sue the insurance companies of their employers, which was far too complicated and time consuming.[177] Even when they became entitled to workman's compensation benefits, farmworkers who lost limbs after getting their hands and arms caught in the machinery often waited for months to receive supplemental income. Charlie White lost a finger during his first week at the Cutchogue labor camp, and Alfonso Terrell, the brother of prizefighter Ernest Terrell, later lost a finger at the same camp. In 1965, Wesley Smith, a migrant worker from a labor camp in Aquebogue, lost a toe while working in a potato grader. In each case, it took several months and assistance from volunteers to finally receive their workman's compensation benefits.

Through the 1980s, agriculture overtook mining as the most dangerous industry in terms of work-related deaths. In 1988, there were ninety-four deaths per one hundred thousand farmworkers against twenty-five deaths per one hundred thousand miners. Since the U.S. Department of Labor did not collect data for farms with fewer than eleven workers, many farmworkers on small Long Island farms were excluded from such surveys. Thus precise statistics for workplace injuries or deaths on Long Island farms might never truly be known.

In an attempt to curb the abysmal health conditions of migratory farmworkers, county officials implemented a series of preventative health care initiatives. In 1956, the Suffolk County Department of Health provided group chest X-rays for workers in ten migrant labor camps in the area.[178] This was an effort to combat tuberculosis and led to a wider program aimed at providing medical and dental care to migrant farmworkers.[179]

In 1962, Health Department doctors assembled in Greenport and conducted a series of tuberculosis tests on migrant workers under the employ of the Eastern Suffolk Cooperative.[180] One year later, Suffolk County legislators received funding for a comprehensive program to provide health services for the thousands of migrant laborers in the county. The cost of the program was estimated to be $255,250, 90 percent of which was paid by federal funds, and included one stationary clinic in Riverhead and a mobile clinic to visit various labor camps.[181] The program also included year-round medical and dental checkups for migrant workers and their families at local doctors and dentists.

Despite the health care initiatives offered by Suffolk County officials on behalf of the migrant workers, the overall health conditions at the migrant labor camps could appropriately be described as poor, and the general lack of adequate health care only compounded the problem and even led to the unnecessary and tragic deaths of several migrant workers.

CRIME AND VIOLENCE

Crime and violence are unavoidable factors in any society. With deplorable living conditions and a ruthlessly exploited and impoverished labor force, it is little wonder that acts of crime and violence emanated from the labor camps as well. "Camp life is lawless," explained Reverend Arthur Bryant. "Rusty guns and shiny knives appear frequently. Police seldom patrol and a number of camps do not even have telephones so that a man may call the cops if he feels that he is being bullied."[182]

Naturally, many of the crimes committed at the camps were motivated by encounters involving money. During the peak of the harvest season, and particularly on Saturday nights when the workers received their weekly pay, fighting, gambling and other acts of disorderly conduct occurred frequently. On September 11, 1948, David Morris stabbed thirty-eight-year-old James Martin in the chest after the two men quarreled over a $5 loan.[183] Both men were migrant workers from the Myron Nelson labor camp on Old Quogue Road in Riverhead. Two months later, William Dorsey, a migrant laborer from another camp in Riverhead, was arrested and charged with second-degree grand larceny for stealing $200 from a car owned by his crew leader.[184] In an extraordinary measure, the prosecuting attorney argued that spending the winter months "in a steam-heated county jail where they receive good, wholesome food, and be released in the spring" was not sufficient punishment, especially at the cost of the taxpayers. Presiding judge D. Ormande Ritchie agreed with the attorney's request and ordered the suspension of any prison sentence on the condition that Dorsey leave the county and never return.

On July 26, 1955, Joseph Bifulco, the president of Local 424 of the International Brotherhood of Teamsters, was attacked by eight migrant workers near the H. Sacks & Sons potato shipping warehouse in Mattituck.[185] The beating occurred after Bifulco stopped to meet with union men who were picketing outside the warehouse. The next day, police arrested Solomon Frank Ballard, a migrant worker from Florida. Ballard admitted to his part in the crime and claimed that the camp's owner, Arnold Sacks, paid the men $100 to beat Bifulco. Mr. Sacks denied the allegations and claimed that he was fishing on the day of the attack. After an investigation, Sacks was cleared of all charges, and Ballard pleaded guilty and was fined $10.[186] A few years later, Phillip Winter, a migrant worker from Riverhead, was charged with larceny when he forged two checks and then attempted to use the funds to purchase a bottle of liquor from a store in Cutchogue.[187]

On September 4, 1957, a particularly frightening encounter occurred when three men raucously entered a labor camp in Greenport demanding liquor and beer. Alberta Holmes, who was a migrant cook at the camp, told the men that they did not serve alcohol, and they abruptly left before returning a few hours later and broke several windows, overturned tables and smashed dishes over her head. When they departed, she notified the police, who searched the area but were unable to locate the trio. A short time later, the men returned, and one of them brandished a gun while the other two seized Ms. Holmes, ripped off her clothes and attempted to rape her. She was able to fight them off and notify the police. She described her assailants as three White men all wearing overalls. The police searched for the men until dark but were unable to locate their whereabouts.[188]

In September 1966, a heinous attack occurred at the Cutchogue labor camp when a laborer named Leroy Anderson threw a chemical solution of bleach and peroxide into the face of Herbert Hawkins, leaving him permanently blind. Police stated that Anderson had been masquerading as a woman at the camp, and Hawkins, who had suspected that Anderson was a man, got into a dispute with him, which led to the attack. Anderson was charged with maiming and faced a maximum sentence of fifteen years in prison.[189]

In 1974, John Earnest, a sixty-seven-year-old crew leader at the Fargo labor camp in Riverhead, was the victim of an early morning mugging.[190] Earnest, who was known to regularly carry large sums of money, was followed and then dragged from his car and robbed of about $300. Two years later, Kirkland Williams, a migrant worker at the Sacks & Sons labor camp, was arrested for attacking another man with a can opener blade and a knife.[191]

At times, certain acts of violence resulted in murder. In October 1947, a twenty-eight-year-old migrant worker named Robert McGriff died of stab wounds from a fellow migrant worker named James Hill at a labor camp in Smithtown. Hill fled the scene but was arrested a short time later when he appeared at another labor camp in East Setauket.[192] In 1955, a migrant farmworker named Willie Patterson was stabbed to death by Eddie G. House at the Cutchogue labor camp. House, who was a laborer from Mississippi and later became known as blues artist Son House, objected when Patterson entered his cabin to search for money that he claimed was owed to him, and House stabbed him in the chest. House fled to the nearby woods but was captured a short while later with the bloody knife in his possession. He later admitted to committing the crime and was arraigned on first-degree manslaughter charges.[193]

One year later, Robert Clayton, a migrant worker at the John Gozelski labor camp in East Northport, was charged for the murder of fellow laborer Candice Nelson.[194] The cause of death was listed as extensive brain hemorrhage induced by multiple skull fractures caused by a blunt instrument. During the trial, prosecutors argued that Clayton killed Nelson for $300 after he had suffered recent gambling losses. One witness testified to having found $260 hidden in a box in his room. In March 1959, a migrant laborer named Jack Wilbur fatally stabbed Hosekiah Harris in the chest with a knife during a drunken brawl at a labor camp in Aquebogue.[195] Wilbur was charged with first-degree manslaughter but was allowed to plead guilty for second-degree assault.

In 1966, a farm laborer named Rogelio Negron stabbed Juan Del Valle to death after the two had an argument at the McKay labor camp on Sound Avenue in Riverhead. Negron was charged with second-degree manslaughter and faced life in prison.[196] One year later, a sixteen-year-old migrant worker named Alfonso McMillan was charged with first-degree manslaughter after he fatally stabbed a fellow migrant worker named Lindberg Brown. The incident occurred after the two were involved in a fight at the I.M. Young labor camp on Youngs Avenue in Southold.[197] In 1974, a migrant laborer was accused of beating another laborer to death after a fight erupted during a poker game. The incident occurred at the Fargo labor camp in Laurel, where the man attacked the victim with his fists and a pool cue. The victim later died from his wounds at a nearby hospital, and the charges were upgraded from assault to murder.[198]

Over the years, there were several gun-related offenses at various labor camps.[199] On September 1, 1947, an altercation occurred between a group of farmworkers at the Cutchogue labor camp. When police arrived, they arrested six men, who later pleaded guilty for possession of unlicensed revolvers. At the same camp a few years later, Nathanial Simms was charged with felonious assault after he shot three workers.[200] Police stated that a large group of the workers were gambling, and when a fight ensued, Simms retrieved a .22-caliber rifle and shot the men.

During the early morning hours of October 6, 1957, David Lee Kendall, a crew leader at the Frank Salters labor camp in Mattituck, was shot and killed by a migrant farmworker at the camp. Witnesses at the scene told police that William Ettison shot Kendall, who was approaching him aggressively with a knife. Ettison fled the scene and was later sought by police in thirteen states.[201] Two years later, Hurley Davis Smith, a farm laborer who was residing in Riverhead, shot and killed another laborer, Johnnie B. James. Smith first attacked James with his fists for failing to clean up after his dog.[202] After the fight, Smith returned with a gun and fatally shot James three times in the chest. Smith, who lived in a run-down home with six children, including a newborn, was charged with first-degree manslaughter. On December 2, 1967, Samuel Seymour Jr., a migrant worker from the I.M. Young labor camp in Southold, was shot twice while walking along Middle Road at 5:30 p.m. Seymour was struck in the arm by two bullets, with one lodging in his lung and the other just an inch above his heart. He told detectives that three White men driving a cream and black sedan cursed at him before firing the shots with a handgun. Seymour was treated at a nearby hospital.[203]

Lastly, in 1970, four individuals were arrested and charged with reckless endangerment for firing weapons, including a semiautomatic rifle, in a field near the Cutchogue labor camp.[204] More than a dozen police officers were dispatched after receiving an anonymous telephone call from a resident who heard the shots. One of the four who were arrested was Arthur Mitchell, who was a student at Stonybrook University. He told police that they were merely engaging in target practice. At the scene, police found newspapers and other paraphernalia from the Black Panthers political group. All four denied any affiliation with the Black Panthers, and Southold police chief Carl Cataldo insisted that the reason for the arrest was for the excessive ammunition found at the scene and not their alleged affiliation with the group.

At times, violence occurred at locations outside of migrant labor camps. In 1946, Joseph Fleming and his brother LeRoy were charged with fatally stabbing a man outside the Blue Bird Inn in Riverhead.[205] According to police, the brothers, who were both laborers at the Hollis Warner duck ranch, entered the bar with a bottle of liquor and began drinking from the bottle. When a man inside objected, tempers flared, and when the three exited the restaurant, the two brothers fatally stabbed the man and were both charged with first-degree murder.

On August 22, 1952, a grower in Cutchogue named Joseph Szawinksi was attacked in his home by an unknown assailant. Szawinski was awakened by a blow to the jaw and was then repeatedly slashed with a knife on his head, stomach, legs and shoulders. The assailant was believed to have been a migrant farmworker at the nearby Cutchogue labor camp. Twenty local police officers searched the camp, and the victim was treated at a nearby hospital.[206]

In a shocking case, the owner of a prominent duck farm was killed by his own son. On August 8, 1967, Hollis Warner, seventy-two, and Rosemary Giles Duff, thirty-one, who were reported to be romantically involved, were shot to death by Warner's own son John Warner, who was upset over their relationship.[207] According to police, Hollis Warner received one gunshot to the head, and Giles, who was a migrant laborer, was shot multiple times in the head, neck, shoulders and arms. John Warner pleaded guilty to reduced charges of first-degree and second-degree manslaughter and was ultimately sentenced to five to fifteen years in Sing Sing Prison in Westchester.[208]

All of these acts of crime and violence were an unfortunate byproduct of the lawless nature of migrant labor camps.

Death at the Camps

The cause and effect of random and deadly acts of violence at the camps generally garnered little public sympathy. However, the deaths of migrant workers at these camps caused by a combination of desperation and negligence could not escape greater public scrutiny. In 1956, local reporter Ruth Schier wrote, "When you crowd people in unsuitable quarters, with inadequate facilities, tragedy is bound to strike, and it did. Even the most hostile communities can no longer feel complacent when they contemplate the charred bodies of children who have been trapped in dwellings away from good water pressure." This chapter explores the tragic events that for many were the sad ending to a troubled life in the migratory labor system of Suffolk County.

On October 8, 1961, a leaky kerosene stove caused a fire at the Cutchogue labor camp and claimed the lives of Leroy McKoy (twenty-three) of South Carolina; James Davis (forty-one) of Baltimore, Maryland; and Charles Jordan (forty-two) of Ravenna, Ohio. The charred bodies of McKoy and Jordan were found in their sleeping quarters, and the body of Davis was found inside after he reportedly reentered the barracks in a desperate attempt to retrieve a new pair of shoes before being overcome by smoke. A fourth man, identified as James Overstreet (twenty-three) of Louisville, Mississippi, was pulled out alive, but he succumbed to his injuries later that day at the nearby Eastern Long Island Hospital.[209] Sixteen other men barely escaped from the one-hundred-by-twenty-five-foot barracks without injury.

Investigators learned that the workers snuck in the cooking stove that caused the fire because they could not afford to pay seventy-five cents for meals at the camp. It was also found that the cooking stove was in the sleeping quarters and not properly secured, which were clear violations of the sanitary code.[210] It was these grim economic conditions that led them to risk and ultimately lose their lives.

Shortly after the fire, health inspectors conducted a thorough inspection at the camp and found it to be inadequately cleaned, maintained or supervised. Senior health inspector Sidney Beckwith stated that the continuance of such conditions "would be just cause to take action to revoke the permit of the camp." Regarding the kerosene stoves, Beckwith added, "These are major violations.…We definitely have, over a period of years, urged the camp to take extra precautions." Assistant District Attorney Ted Jaffe stated that there was no criminal liability for the fire. However, he cited the "disgraceful conditions" of the camp and added that "there is an air of general sloppiness about the place."[211]

The Cutchogue labor camp garnered a great amount of public attention. However, little would change, and the fatalities continued. Just seven weeks later, on November 24, 1961, James Harris suffocated to death in a shack fire that erupted after a kerosene heater exploded.[212] The forty-year-old Harris was a migrant laborer on the Anthony Babinski farm on Mecox Road in Bridgehampton. Assistant Suffolk County district attorney Anthony Theodore stated, "There's nothing that can be done to eliminate these tragedies unless the farmers and labor camp operators regulate themselves."

On January 27, 1963, a fire tore through a slum-like shack at the Stanco labor camp in East Hampton during the early morning hours, killing five children.[213] The cause of the fire was a defective flue on a kerosene heater. The four-room shack on Gardiner Avenue was inhabited by Jeremiah and Eleanor Williams, who watched helplessly as their children Brenda (six), Michael (five), Barbara Jane (two) and Jerri (three months) perished inside, and their one-year-old daughter, Jacqueline, died at Southampton Hospital later that day. The building inspector for East Hampton had just visited the home three days earlier and considered condemning the building immediately but added, "What do you do with the seven human beings you toss out on the street?"

On January 14, 1968, a fire erupted at the dilapidated Jacobs labor camp in Bridgehampton, killing Myrtle Lee Grant (forty-five), James Farrell (forty) and his wife, Gussie Mae Farrell (thirty-five).[214] Three others were injured and fourteen barely escaped injury in the blaze that was caused by a faulty kerosene stove used for heat. Police investigated and discovered that the door of the room where the victims were found was nailed shut, reportedly to keep out the cold draft. Mr. Jacobs was arrested and later freed on $600 bail. A local grower, William Sayre, who regularly visited the home to collect the rent, blamed the deaths on the occupants. Alex Gartner, the director of the Economic Opportunity Council, sharply criticized Sayre's comments, stating, "Mr. Sayre illustrates the kind of inhumanity brought about by the type of farm labor system we tolerate."

There were other dangers inherent in the migratory labor system. The men, woman and children farmworkers who were transported as far as two thousand miles north across various states endured long and uncomfortable rides with brief stops made only for meals and restroom breaks. In the documentary *Harvest of Shame*, workers were filmed boarding overcrowded trucks and being driven to North Carolina, Virginia, Maryland, Delaware,

Top: Migrant farmworkers boarding a truck in 1942 near Bridgeton, New Jersey, to work in the fields. *Courtesy of the Library of Congress.*

Bottom: Migrant farmworkers crowded on a truck in 1942. The low height of the side rails posed a serious danger to the occupants. *Courtesy of the Library of Congress.*

New Jersey and on to Long Island and upstate New York. The customary vehicles used were "old, stake-type trucks, fitted with board benches."[215] Later, makeshift buses were used.

These trips occasionally ended in tragedy. On June 6, 1957, twenty-one migrant workers, including a baby, were killed when the truck they were traveling in near Fayetteville, North Carolina, collided with another vehicle. Passenger overcrowding was deemed to be one of the causes of the accident.[216] At the time of the accident, there were only six states that had strict laws that required the safe transportation of migrant workers in their borders. The state of North Carolina was not one of those.

In 1963, twenty-seven Mexican migrant workers were killed when a makeshift bus they were riding in was ripped apart by a crossing freight train in Salinas, California.[217] One year later, a bus traveling from Delaware to Maryland crashed and killed six Puerto Rican farmworkers and injured another twenty-two.[218] A few years later, nine migrant workers were killed, including two young children, and another sixteen were injured when the bus they were riding on collided with a train at an intersection in the small town of Newtonville, New Jersey.[219] The crossing had no lights or barriers. While these fatal accidents occurred in locations outside of Long Island, many of these migrant workers traveled similar routes and faced the same dangerous conditions.

In Suffolk County, there were several auto accidents involving migrant workers that led to serious injury and even death. On September 5, 1946, Richard Knowles, a twenty-one-year-old migrant worker at a labor camp in Kings Park, was seriously injured after being thrown from a farm vehicle

Migrant farmworkers boarding a truck in 1940, which will take them from Belcross, North Carolina, to work on a farm at Onley, Virginia. *Courtesy of the Library of Congress.*

that abruptly swerved to avoid an oncoming car. Mr. Knowles was thrown from the vehicle in such a way that the rear wheels ran over his body. He suffered fractures of the skull, spine and left leg, and his right leg had to be amputated just below the knee.[220]

In 1954, George T. Jordan, a migrant laborer, was killed, and three others were badly injured in an automobile accident in East Northport.[221] Just one month later, several migrant workers from the Long Island Produce labor camp in Bridgehampton were involved in a car crash that killed three of them instantly and left five more fighting for their lives.[222] In 1960, fifty-one-year-old Edward Millen was struck and killed by a car while trying to cross Montauk Highway in Bridgehampton.[223] Millen had arrived from South Carolina just three weeks earlier and was a worker at the H. Sacks & Sons labor camp. Lastly, during a foggy morning on November 7, 1978, a truck traveling west on Route 58 in Riverhead collided with a car, which then struck a bus being driven by Carl Beamon, who was transporting twenty-six migrant workers to his labor camp in Calverton. None of the passengers on the bus were seriously injured.[224]

Migrant farmworkers in Suffolk County were beleaguered with isolation, degradation, dependency and exploitation. Their lives were riddled with poor health and besieged in a setting rife with crime and violence. The horrific deaths of men, women and children in dangerous shacks, barracks or other squalid dwellings, along with the inherent dangers involved in the transportation to and from the labor camps, have all come to shape the dismal and often tragic life of migrant workers in Suffolk County during the twentieth century.

CALL TO ACTION

Enforcement

Ever since the first labor camp was opened in Suffolk County, health department inspectors and local law enforcement officers were tasked with performing routine inspections to ensure compliance with state laws. Local officials pledged their full support for these inspections.[225] In 1952, the Suffolk County Board of Supervisors reviewed numerous inspection reports and stated that "conditions at migrant labor camps are detrimental to camp occupants and the community alike." As a result, the group unanimously adopted a resolution that declared that it is "the policy of the Board to support the various county agencies in their enforcement of the regulations and laws regarding migrant labor activities."

One year later, the town board of Brookhaven considered stronger measures to curb what it called the "constant menace" at the labor camps in the township.[226] The proposed regulations required anyone establishing a camp to post a cash bond. The camps also had to meet building and health standards; provide sanitary facilities, running water and electricity; and be placed at certain distances away from homes. However, the measure was placed on hold, as the town attorney was required to review the legality of the bond requirement. Later in the year, calls continued to be made for more stringent enforcement of the labor camps in Brookhaven.

Enforcement of the sanitary code at the labor camps proved to be quite challenging. Camp owners were often made aware of the scheduled inspections ahead of time and thus had to time to correct any potential violations, only to allow the camp to fall into disrepair afterward. Moreover, since the burden of proof rested with the county, violations were difficult to prosecute. This often led to delays and multiple court adjournments. Cases that were extended beyond the harvest season were often withdrawn or dismissed for lack of sufficient evidence or available witnesses.

Despite these challenges, inspectors achieved a fair amount of success over the years. In 1949, Suffolk County health commissioner Dr. Philip Rafle and a team of building inspectors toured five different labor camps in the town of Brookhaven.[227] Although they found no serious hazards, Dr. Rafle stressed that some camps needed improvement. One of the sites they visited was the Bruno Beck labor camp in Port Jefferson, and they reported that "some of the camp facilities are not properly maintained" and that the camp was "being operated without competent supervision."

The Stanley Detmers labor camp in East Setauket was also thoroughly inspected and described as "passable," and while the Peters labor camp in Gordon Heights was deemed to be "generally satisfactory," the inspectors did recommend more adequate water supply and improved toilet facilities. A labor camp near the Still Farm in Coram was found to be in poor condition, but since it was registered as a boardinghouse at the time, it did not fall within their jurisdiction. Lastly, the group visited the Nowaski labor camp in Miller Place, where a tent was erected and used to house fourteen migrant workers. Sanitary conditions at this location were described as "primitive" and in violation of the zoning ordinance. It was ordered to be immediately shut down.

In 1957, two camp operators named Benjamin Halsey and John Henry Coty pleaded guilty for operating labor camps in Northampton in violation of state health laws. Investigators found twenty-nine people living in buildings littered with garbage and sharing a filthy bathroom, and there was an overflowing cesspool in the yard where young children played. Halsey paid a twenty-five-dollar fine and promised to shut down his camp, while Coty paid a ten-dollar fine, and as a condition to remain in operation, he was required to clear up the violations.[228]

The passage of sweeping new laws both in 1954 and 1958 strengthened the state's sanitary code and ushered in a new era of stricter regulations at migrant labor camps throughout New York. Empowered with more authority to issue steeper penalties for violators, state officials were finally positioned to administer enhanced oversight at the camps. In Suffolk County, senior health department inspector Sidney Beckwith publicly announced the new

NEW YORK STATE DEPARTMENT OF HEALTH
MIGRANT LABOR CAMP INSPECTION REPORT

NAME AND ADDRESS	TOWN OR VILLAGE	COUNTY	CAPACITY	NO. OCCUPANTS

(Form filled in handwriting: Beamon Camp, Riverhead — Riverhead — Suff — 031 — M F C, etc.)

Above: A copy of an inspection report at the Carl Beamon labor camp in Riverhead, New York, dated November 28, 1988. To the right and under the comment titled "Remarks," the inspectors listed the violations that needed to be remedied. At the top right, under the number of occupants, the report listed eight male workers and two female workers at the camp. *Courtesy of the Library of the Suffolk County Department of Health.*

Opposite: A copy of an inspection report at the I.M. Young labor camp in Cutchogue, New York, dated November 17, 1988. James Wilson was the camp operator who was interviewed during this inspection. *Courtesy of the Library of the Suffolk County Department of Health.*

NEW YORK STATE DEPARTMENT OF HEALTH
MIGRANT LABOR CAMP INSPECTION REPORT

NAME AND ADDRESS	TOWN OR VILLAGE	COUNTY	CAPACITY	NO. OCCUPANTS

I M Young Cutchogue — Southold — Suff

0 2 5 1 8 0 2 — PRE SEASON 1, MID SEASON 2, POST SEASON 3 — DATE 1 1 1 7 8 0

REMARKS (List by numbers):

81 – one of three toilets at north end of bldg. does not flush.

37 – broken window pane in toilet room at north end of bldg.

81 – shower stall currently in use shall be thoroughly cleaned & resurf.

36 – some interior painting needed especially metal casement awning windows.

53, 54 – kerosene in can w/ pump noted in store room – storage of fuel & unvented heat not permitted

Person interviewed and title: Mr. Wilson

Where interviewed: camp — Date interviewed: 11/17

Inspected by: R H. Gerdts — Date inspected: 11/17

rules and warned all camp owners in the county of upcoming inspections prior to and throughout each harvest season.[229] In 1958, there were 2,334 camp inspections throughout the county, which was significantly greater that the 1,176 inspections in 1951.[230] By 1967, health inspectors visited the camps at a minimum of once per month.[231]

Over the years, the inspections at the labor camps appear to have been carried out more thoroughly. According to the New York State Department of Health Migrant Labor Camp Inspection Report, officials followed a forty-seven-point checklist while inspecting migrant labor camps. It included items such as housing and sanitation, cooking areas and responsibilities of the occupants at the camp.[232] By 1985, the report form was expanded to a seventy-seven-point inspection, which added specified sections for fire safety, water supply and toilets. Camp owners were typically given one week to clear up the violations. Serious violations or a failure to correct violations in a timely manner led to the issuance of immediate fines, other penalties and possibly even jail time.

Despite the new rules and greater oversight, some camp owners appeared to act with impunity. In 1967, Henry Jacobs, the owner of the notorious Jacobs labor camp on Foster Avenue in Bridgehampton, was charged with a multitude of violations at the camp, which included inadequate heating, improper sanitary facilities and untended garbage. Just six months later, three migrant farmworkers were killed by fire at this same camp.[233] Jacobs was arrested and later freed on $600 bail.[234] However, as he awaited trial, he died from complications after undergoing abdominal surgery, and the case was dropped.[235]

One year later, Joseph Borella, the owner of a migrant labor camp on Moriches Road in Brookhaven, was cited for eleven violations of the sanitary code, including poor sanitary facilities and operating the camp without a proper permit.[236] Each charge was a misdemeanor and subjected him to fines and imprisonment of up to six months. Borella received similar violations in 1963 and 1965, respectively, but in both cases, the charges were dismissed for lack of evidence because it was the end of the harvest season and the migrant workers had already moved out of the camp.

In January 1970, representatives of the Suffolk County Department of Health shut down the Cutchogue labor camp because of numerous sanitation violations, along with inadequate carpentry, heating and plumbing.[237] At the time, there were seventeen migrant workers and four young children at the camp. Faced with criminal prosecution if he attempted to remain open, camp operator Herbert Cassidy evicted the migrant workers. One year later, Suffolk County conducted a survey of inspections at all seventy-nine registered labor camps in the county. According to the survey, health inspectors found 965 sanitary and housing violations.[238] Of the inspections conducted over the year, at least one violation was found in each camp. Seventeen of the camps were found to have a rat infestation, and all of the camps were ordered to undertake pest and rodent extermination measures.

On September 26, 1972, the Suffolk County Migratory Affairs Council was established to investigate, make recommendations and promote health, welfare and safety standards in the farming community and at the migrant labor camps.[239] A man named Lawrence Stewart, from Westhampton Beach, was selected for the position. Once in charge, Stewart led a series of surprise inspections at various migrant labor camps throughout the county. In 1975, a surprise inspection led to the arrest of camp operators Lee Washington, from the Bushwick labor camp in Jamesport, and Ernest Mitchell, from the Fargo labor camp in Laurel. Both men were charged with more than twenty violations at each of the camps, which included severe overcrowding and the illegal sale of liquor.[240] All of the charges were misdemeanors punishable by fines of up to $500. Stewart stated, "The camps were filthy and overcrowded and Mitchell was selling pints of wine worth 69 cents for $2 and charging 85 cents for a pack of cigarettes." Mitchell was also charged with beating a migrant worker and stealing money and shoes from two other workers. Later that year, Wilson Liles, the operator of the Pollack labor camp on Edgar Avenue in Riverhead, was arrested on six charges of violating the public health law.[241] The charges included the operation of the camp without a permit, along with providing inadequate bedding, fire extinguishers and screens.

Several years after his previous arrest, Ernest Mitchell was operating a labor camp in Riverhead when he was charged with tax evasion.[242] At the trial, witnesses testified that Mitchell cheated his workers by forcing them to sign receipts for more pay than they actually received, and he charged them $20 per week for food and lodging. Other witnesses testified that he paid $500 a month to rent the camp barracks from the farm owner and received $400 to $500 per week on the money he collected from the workers. Mitchell never properly reported his earnings and faced a maximum of twenty-four years in prison and a fine of $80,000. While this case was considered successful, it took two and a half years to investigate and prosecute.

In 1975, a series of inspections occurred at various labor camps in Bridgehampton. Local police and inspectors raided the H. Sacks & Sons labor camp and charged camp operator Zack Wright with eight violations of the sanitary code. Just one month before, this same camp was cited for operating without a permit.[243] Sinclair T. Smith of the Baldwin labor camp was charged with ten violations, and Ruby Dell Jenkins was charged with operating a commissary at that camp without a license.[244] Operators of the South Shore Produce labor camp and the Wesnofske labor camp were also cited for minor violations as a result of the crackdown.

In response to his zealous efforts to curb the deplorable conditions of the many labor camps, Lawrence Stewart received anonymous death threats.[245] Even Stewart's wife feared danger, which was evident one day when she was driving along a road in Westhampton Beach and heard what she thought was the sound of a bullet striking her car. Local police investigated and found a small hole in the windshield, which they believed came from a pebble that flew up from the road. Despite concerns for the safety of his family, Mr. Stewart defiantly proclaimed, "There are more inspections planned for the near future. I've been charged with the responsibility of cleaning up this mess and I'm going to do it."

In 1977, Stewart and two state troopers raided the Bolling labor camp on Queen Street in Greenport. After the inspection, they cited operator Charles C. Whatley and a bookkeeper at the camp with numerous violations of the sanitary and health codes. In the trial for this case, prosecutors argued that because the presiding judge, Southold Town justice Louis Demarest, was a potato grower himself and part of the same farmer association as the owner of the Bolling camp, he should recuse himself from the case.[246] Judge Demarest refused that request, presided over the case and dismissed all charges. In a stunning turn of events, the defendants filed a $500,000 lawsuit against Stewart and Suffolk County, alleging that they illegally entered the private property of the camp. Simon Perchik, the assistant district attorney who handled the complaint, argued that the lawsuit was frivolous and that its sole purpose was to create a chilling effect on the enforcement of the laws designed to inspect the labor camps.[247]

Finally, in 1982, state supreme court justice William Underwood signed an order to close the Bolling labor camp in Greenport.[248] Earlier in the month, the camp was cited for seventeen violations, including the operation of the camp without a permit, litter and debris on the property, unsanitary bedding for the workers, unventilated heaters and a lack of hot or cold water. One inspector stated that the residents of the camp lived in "deplorable conditions." As a result of the inspection, Bolling was fined $3,000, which at the time was the largest monetary fine ever issued to a migrant labor camp operator. After Mr. Bolling failed to comply with the order to remedy the violations, the court ordered the camp to be permanently closed.

Inspectors of the Suffolk County Office of Migrant Affairs, along with health department and other county officials, were beset with limited resources and, at times, were subjected to threats and lawsuits simply for doing their jobs. Their role of inspecting and successfully enforcing the laws at the numerous labor camps was a very daunting task. Nonetheless, their efforts intensified over the years, particularly after the passage of the new laws, and they held to account the camp operators who shirked the health and sanitary laws governing the migrant labor camps. Those who did violate the laws paid stiffer penalties, both monetarily and judicially, and some camps were forced to close for noncompliance. These enforcement efforts played a vital role in the fight against the wretched conditions of the migrant labor camps.

Judicial Intervention

Migrant labor camps throughout the country were typically situated in relative isolation miles from the nearest towns. They were often encircled in barbed wire and dotted with no trespassing signs.[249] Camp operators and crew leaders were greatly agitated by organizers, reporters, lawyers and civil rights activists who attempted to visit and report the conditions of the camps. Shootings and other acts of violence were not uncommon. In 1972, Geraldo Rivera reported on various migrant labor camps for an *Eyewitness News* special titled "Migrants Dirt Cheap." While the crew was attempting to film the conditions of a labor camp at the Shuback Farm in Orange County, New York, they became entrapped by several growers who blocked the road with their cars. A tense standoff ensued, and one grower attacked one of the cameramen, forcing Rivera to momentarily subdue the assailant. Shortly afterward, another man reached into their car to attack one of the crew members as they drove onto the grass to escape the farm.

In Suffolk County, visitors and so-called do-gooders who attempted to meet with migrant workers were typically met with disdain from the growers, camp operators and crew leaders. This often led to dramatic and occasionally violent showdowns. In 1954, Jesse Morgan, a mechanic from New York City, visited Cutchogue equipped with a camera to film the conditions at the labor camp on Cox Lane. Someone at the camp spotted him and immediately notified the police. When they arrived, an altercation ensued, and Morgan, who was a Black man, allegedly called one of the White troopers an obscenity. In response, Morgan, who was wearing a surgical back brace from a previous automobile accident, was struck in the back with a nightstick and collapsed in pain. He was taken to Eastern Long Island Hospital in nearby Greenport.[250]

Three days later, the troopers went to the hospital and arrested Morgan, who was transported on a stretcher to appear before the Mattituck justice of the peace, Ralph W. Tuthill. The courtroom was the kitchen of Tuthill's home. Morgan was represented by Jawn Sandifer, who was a civil rights lawyer and official of the NAACP who would later become a New York State judge. The prosecution was led by William J. Lindsay, an aide for the district attorney who was not an attorney. Court transcripts revealed that several times throughout the trial, Lindsay shouted at defense attorney Sandifer to "sit down" and to "be quiet." At one point, Sandifer objected to the presentation of certain evidence from the arresting officer, and Lindsay stated to the judge, "It's all right to use that." Judge Tuthill ultimately ruled against Morgan and charged him with disorderly conduct. Morgan immediately filed an appeal and a separate lawsuit against the county for $25,000 for the injuries he sustained in the altercation with the police.

The appeal was heard by Judge Fred J. Munder. Sandifer protested the misconduct of the investigator for the prosecution who "took over" the proceedings. "Never in my experience as a practicing attorney have I ever had anything like this happen," said Sandifer. After portions of the transcript were read in open court, even the Suffolk County district attorney admitted that the investigator clearly "overstepped his duties and his responsibility." The prosecution requested a new trial while the defense argued for a dismissal of all the charges. Judge Munder dismissed the charges against Morgan but ordered a new trial to be heard by a different justice of the peace.[251] This entire chain of events erupted merely because Morgan attempted to photograph conditions at the labor camp.

Over the years, inspectors from the Suffolk County Health Department were also subjected to threats of violence from labor camp owners or operators. In one case in 1968, George Szczepanowski, a cucumber grower in Bridgehampton, was charged with assaulting two health department inspectors who cited him for operating a labor camp without a permit.[252] Mr. Szczepanowski was required to a pay a $250 fine, and his camp was shut down, which forced him to abandon his pickle crop for the season.

Members of the press were also targeted for violence. On September 15, 1971, a local assemblyman, Andrew Stein, and a local reporter, Karl Grossman, visited the Cutchogue labor camp. Stein toured the camp and openly criticized the treatment of the migrant workers. "The conditions here are feudal," Stein stated. "People live like indentured servants. This is not the kind of thing we want in New York."[253] As Stein was speaking with a migrant worker, William Chudiak, the president of the Eastern

Suffolk Farmer's Cooperative, attacked Grossman with a piece of wood and threatened other members of Stein's team. "He went after my camera first," stated Grossman, "and then hit me over the head with a two by four piece of wood and busted my head wide open."[254] The attack left Grossman badly injured; however, he declined to press criminal charges. Over the years, various state officials, reporters and civil rights advocates who attempted to visit labor camps allegedly received warnings of physical violence and even death threats from camp owners, operators and crew leaders.

For years, civil rights advocates contested the growers' interference with visitors at migrant labor camps. They argued that migrant workers had a constitutional right to welcome visitors seeking to assist them. In 1971, the American Civil Liberties Union (ACLU) embarked on a national project to bring test cases to federal courts involving access to labor camps.[255] ACLU attorney Burt Nueborne told reporters that six lawsuits were filed to cover labor camps in various geographical areas, including Suffolk County. Nueborne, who was once threatened by a grower near Bridgehampton who fired gun shots over his head, added that the suits were intended to challenge the growers' use of criminal trespass laws to restrict visitors from their farms, including public officials, union organizers and reporters.

William Chudiak, the same grower who just three months later would attack Karl Grossman at the Cutchogue labor camp, criticized the initiative and proclaimed that many of the growers would simply quit farming if migrant workers could join unions. "I don't care what they do," Chudiak stated. "I don't have to farm, but you people have to eat. That's something you should think about....This project is being pushed by the Communist Party....People think we can grow things for nothing. It's not the better wages we oppose, it's the people who are working for them. If you don't push them all the time, they won't do a damn thing."

Later that year in Grand Rapids, Michigan, U.S. district judge Noel P. Fox ordered a grower to pay $4,500 in damages for interfering with visitors in one of the migrant labor camps.[256] In the landmark ruling, Judge Fox stated that "property ownership does not vest the owner with dominion over the lives of people living on his property. The migrants who travel across the country to work in the grower's fields and live on the grower's property are clothed with their full bundle of rights as citizens and human beings. They may not be held in servitude or peonage, and they are not serfs."

The court's ruling, along with other related cases, was the first to establish a constitutional right of access to migrant labor camps for all law-abiding, nonprofit visitors, including labor union organizers, reporters and other human rights advocates. Thus, by law, visitors could no longer be barred from labor camps. As a result, there was heightened exposure at the migrant labor camps, which was a critical factor in the fight against poor conditions and abuse of farmworkers.

Advocacy

The economic exploitation and poor conditions of the migrant labor camps in Suffolk County were met with fierce resistance from individuals, along with religious and social justice groups seeking reform. One of the first known examples of this community advocacy came in the wake of the death of two young children who were burned to death in a Bridgehampton migrant shack in 1949. This tragedy spurred the community to devise a way to protect the children of migrant workers.[257] Dr. H. Binga Dismond, a prominent Black doctor from nearby Sag Harbor, agreed to rent a house that he owned on Sag Harbor Turnpike for a nominal fee to be used as a childcare center.[258] After the selection of a board of directors, the Bridgehampton Child Care and Recreation Center was established.

Two years later, a larger facility was procured through the generosity of Mrs. Charles F. Brush, who purchased a six-and-a-half-acre property between Bridgehampton and Sag Harbor Roads.[259] For a small fee, up to sixty children of migrant workers were provided with care and meals while their parents worked in the fields. One advertisement for the center read, "The people of Bridgehampton feel that this project will be a big step toward improving the deplorable conditions of the migrant laborer, which is a shameful problem in our country, in this day of the 'Higher Standard of Living for the American Worker.'"

New York State subsidized 75 percent of the center's operating expenses, and area volunteers held fundraisers for material and equipment. The center also had the full support of area artists, who held benefit events at nearby beaches, called the Art on the Dunes, to raise money for the program.[260] Toy drives, music festivals and other events were also held in support of the center. Later, a sizeable federal grant was secured for adult and child literacy initiatives, preschool and after-school day care and teenage youth development programs, which provided job referrals, college advisory services and recreational facilities.[261] The Bridgehampton Child Care Center was a tremendous success and still serves its community as of this writing.

Various religious groups also advocated for improved conditions at the labor camps. In 1949, the Protestant Church announced a ten-year plan on behalf of migrant workers nationwide.[262] Locally, Reverend Austin H. Armistead, a Methodist pastor, spent five years following the migrant stream from Florida to Long Island, where he provided counseling, community entertainment, religious services and educational programs for migrant workers. In 1952, Armistead spoke at a public meeting in Center Moriches, where he advocated for a mutually constructive approach to help both the migrant workers and the growers throughout the county.[263]

In 1956, the Suffolk County–based Council of Churches Committee for Migrant Work held a fundraiser for the establishment of a program called "Harvester of the Migrant Ministry." The money was needed to purchase a New Englander Harvester station wagon that was used as a mobile church. The vehicle was fully equipped with an altar, organ, movie projector, library, sporting equipment and other items intended to bring worship and recreation to migrant workers in many of the labor camps.[264] The program began in 1947, when the first in a fleet of station wagons was deployed to the Cutchogue labor camp.[265]

Over the years, certain individuals spent an enormous amount of time and energy advocating for migrant workers. In 1956, a woman named Helen Gray Smith received the Man of the Year award from the Kiwanis Club of Huntington for her activities with the Migrant Workers Committee.[266] Through her efforts, migrant workers obtained the services of chaplains to help guide those with poor living conditions. In her acceptance speech for the award, which was typically awarded to a man, Smith cautioned against complacency to the migrant worker problem and stated, "The problem throughout Suffolk County, the richest farm producing county in the state, still remains and will for many years to come." She stressed the need for more ministers to help migrant families in need.

There were few individuals in Suffolk County who could match the level of advocacy on behalf of the migrant workers more than Reverend Arthur C. Bryant. In 1958, Bryant accepted a call to service in St. Peter's Lutheran Church in Greenport and the Advent Lutheran Church in Mattituck. Since his arrival, Bryant inspired his parishioners to volunteer for programs to help migrant workers. He also coordinated with other religious groups to invite local politicians to the area to discuss the migrant worker situation and even attempted, albeit unsuccessfully, a campaign to have migrant workers join the United Auto Workers union.[267]

Above and opposite: Mobile church services provided by the Suffolk County Council of Churches at the Cutchogue labor camp in Cutchogue, New York, beginning in 1947. The vehicle contained a portable organ and various recreational items for the children at the camp. *Courtesy of the Southold Historical Society, Southold, New York.*

Reverend Bryant also served as the vice chairman of the Suffolk County Human Relations Commission, an unpaid volunteer position. During his tenure, he gathered petitions with thousands of signatures and sent over two thousand letters to New York State legislators advocating for the inclusion of farmworkers in the New York Labor Relations Act. He also called for the extension of workmen's compensation benefits, higher wages and access to health care for migrant workers.[268] The commission also advocated for written labor contracts that would provide a minimum wage increase and for migrant workers to be paid during work stoppages at no fault of their own.

Under Bryant's leadership, the commission staunchly advocated for the adoption of a stricter state health code to help remedy the abysmal conditions at the labor camps. Specifically, the group proposed more adequate living space with single and double rooms instead of the typical bullpen-style sleeping quarters, along with the installation of telephones at all camps.

The group also protested a decision by the New York State Division of Housing and Community Renewal to exclude seasonal farmworkers from the state's Transient Housing Model Code, which provided minimum state requirements for the living conditions of all transient workers. They believed that this exclusion was discriminatory to the bulk of the migrant workforce, who were primarily Black and Puerto Rican farmworkers.[269]

The commission described the migratory labor system as "corrupt and brutal" and condemned the typical crew leader as "a law to himself" who sells foodstuff, tobacco and alcohol at markup rates of up to 100 percent. The group also advocated for the creation of rehabilitation centers to combat the rampant alcohol abuse in the camps. Ultimately, it urged county executive Lee Dennison to draft a comprehensive plan to abolish the migratory labor system in Suffolk County within one year.[270] Dennison, who had previously called for the elimination of the system himself, promised to review their recommendations.

Bryant's actions were met with outrage by many growers and industry officials, who vigorously condemned any change that infringed on their farm labor needs.[271] Richard Carey, vice president of the Lipco-Agway labor camp in Riverhead, commented, "If migrants are abolished what would they do for work? In my 35 years' experience, I have never seen the time when local help was sufficient. If the migrants go, who will do the work?" Another grower, who refused to be identified, stated, "If they go, everyone in Suffolk, Dennison and Hanse [county board chairman] too, had better learn to eat grass."

In 1969, the growers formed a so-called Truth Squad to address what they argued were distortions made by Bryant and other "do-gooders."[272] They also circulated a petition to block Reverend Bryant's reappointment to the Suffolk County Human Relations Commission. Labor union leaders and civil rights groups vigorously protested this petition and pledged their full support for Bryant. Thelma Drew, vice president of the Smithtown branch of the NAACP, stated, "He's doing a marvelous job and he's doing it on a voluntary basis." The group threatened to picket the homes of local politicians if Bryant was not allowed to continue in his role with the commission. Undeterred by the threat, Reverend Bryant stated, "Some things were bitterly resented. Nobody resented the death of three migrants in Bridgehampton, but they resented the talk about it." Eventually, Reverend Bryant retained his position, and in summing up the controversy, he stated, "It is an open question whether an unpaid position of a Human Rights Commission makes me a civil servant or civil enemy."[273]

On June 9, 1969, Reverend Bryant appeared in Washington, D.C., to testify before a senate committee on migratory labor. He was joined by the producers of the documentary *What Harvest for the Reaper?*, which was released one year earlier. Together they presented the documentary to the committee and submitted supporting documents detailing the conditions of the camps in Suffolk County.

(*Left*): Reverend Arthur Bryant in Greenport, New York, 1963. *Courtesy Personal Collection.*

(*Right*): Reverend Arthur Bryant in Vandalia, Illinois, 1972. *Courtesy of Leader-Union Publishing Co., Vandalia, Illinois.*

During the hearing, Arthur Bryant delivered a compelling speech, titled "Powerlessness," that articulated the physical and psychological plight of migrant workers and the conditions they faced at labor camps on Long Island. Bryant, who was a former commercial fisherman, urged the lawmakers to extend the labor rights provided under the National Labor Relations Act to the nation's agricultural workers, stating:

> *I see no essential difference between agricultural workers and fishermen in their right to strike at harvest time so that life is shown to be more important than food. I remember my 10 friends who sunk on the hulk called the* Gayhead *and the 11 men who went down on the* Margie *and* Pat *which was held together with guy wires. I see no difference between them and the migrants who burn in shacks, who drink for relief from physical and nutritional torture, who knows the loneliness of life without a family. I am a fisherman and I had the Labor Relations Act to protect me. When I walk into a migrant camp, I am reliving my past. But I had a way out. I am an American and so I have rights. My farm labor friends, Myrtle Grant, James Bittle, Alf Terell, Jubilee, and James McNeil should have rights too. We are all Americans. Can't we ensure that no brother is entitled to less opportunity than we have?*

The group delivered a compelling presentation and ultimately brought a relatively unknown and local problem into the national spotlight.

On September 27, 1970, Arthur Bryant was honored by the Suffolk County chapter of the New York Civil Liberties Union for his tireless work on behalf of migrant workers in the county. He continued with his staunch advocacy until his departure from Long Island in 1971, when he and his family relocated to Illinois. One year later, the Suffolk County Migratory Affairs Council was established to promote the health, welfare and safety standards in the farming community.[274] The group also conducted investigations at the labor camps and made recommendations to remedy the "dehumanizing effect" on the migrant farmworkers by the crew leaders who exploit them.

Another fierce advocate on behalf of farmworkers was Mary Chase Stone, founder of Long Island Volunteers, a nonprofit group based in Riverhead. In 1965, Mrs. Stone applied for a federal grant under the Migrant Program provision of the Economic Opportunity Act and was awarded with $203,663 in aid, making it the first volunteer group on Long Island to receive federal funding for a migrant program.[275] This paved the way for other groups to secure critical funding needed to address various social justice issues. Stone also embarked on a judicial crusade with her group to bring corrupt crew leaders and camp operators to justice in several cases, including the 1972 prosecution of crew leader James L. Brown of the Sacks and Sons Potato processing plant in Mattituck.[276] She also assisted in the prosecution of James Covil and Ernest Mitchell, two corrupt crew leaders.

The group established the Long Island Volunteers Boxing Club in Riverhead, which provided underprivileged teens an opportunity to train with boxing star Benjamin Butler and learn the aspects of the sport. The program produced local champions of various age groups who participated in the Golden Gloves boxing tournament throughout the New York area.[277] Stone also helped organize the nonprofit group Seasonal Employees and Agriculture, which was later directed by Raymond Nelson, a lifelong resident of Riverhead and U.S. Air Force veteran. Under Nelson's leadership, the group provided self-improvement courses for migrant farmworkers to learn various trades, such as auto mechanics, carpentry, construction, adult literacy and family life.[278]

A federal volunteer program also aided in the advocacy of migrant workers. In 1964, and in the spirit of President Johnson's war on poverty initiative, Congress enacted the Economic Opportunity Act, which contained a provision for a domestic peace corps called the Volunteers in Service to America (VISTA).[279] Suffolk County officials applied to the program for VISTA volunteers to assist by living and working among migrant workers at various labor camps to gain a better understanding of how to remedy the conditions there. A short time later, the first VISTA volunteers arrived and began to provide these critical services at the Cutchogue labor camp and other camps in the area.[280] VISTA volunteers also provided a wide range of self-help services to underprivileged residents of the North Fork area, which included tutoring at the Greenport school and other programs, such as health, education, recreation, medical care and house painting projects.

One local group provided valuable services to the North Fork community and continues to do so as of this writing. In the early 1960s, Southold supervisor Lester Albertson gathered local clergymen, including Reverend Ben Burns from Southold and Arthur Bryant from Greenport, to discuss the dire conditions of impoverished families and migrant farmworkers on the North Fork. They received federal funding to establish the Community Action Southold Town (CAST). By 1965, CAST had established a board of directors and enlisted volunteers, including a twenty-five-year-old mother of six children named Bessie Swann, who later stated, "CAST was the network

Above: Migrant workers in the 1970s gathered at the headquarters of the Seasonal Employees in Agriculture in Riverhead, New York, for some much-needed recreation. *Courtesy of Raymond Nelson.*

Left: Migrant workers in the 1970s gathered at the headquarters of the Seasonal Employees in Agriculture in Riverhead, New York, for training in construction and various other trades. A large part of the group's mission was to train workers in other trades so that they could leave the migrant stream and find more reliable work. *Courtesy of Raymond Nelson.*

Above: Cinder blocks and cement work being taught to migrant workers at the headquarters of the Seasonal Employees in Agriculture. *Photos courtesy of Raymond Nelson.*

Right: Raymond Nelson, lifelong resident of Riverhead, New York, veteran of the United States Air Force and former director of Seasonal Agriculture in Employment. *Courtesy of Mark Torres.*

that helped so many people overcome serious conditions and poverty in that community, not only through financial help, but through advocacy and political support." CAST also coordinated with VISTA volunteers to assist migrant workers from various labor camps and lobbied prominent politicians like Robert F. Kennedy to sponsor reforms at the Cutchogue labor camp.[281] Later, the group established programs that included literacy assistance, legal aid, job placement and childcare.[282]

For more than half a century, CAST has been providing vital services to the most impoverished families on the North Fork. Some of the programs include a food pantry, a "sharing room," ESL classes, tutoring and mentoring services for school-age children, the Feed-A-Kid program, a school supply drive, summer story hours and a holiday gift program. This grassroots organization is a shining beacon of charity that provides vital necessities to the underserved who reside in one of the most affluent counties in New York.

Finally, although federal and state law specifically denied farmworkers the right to collectively bargain or join a labor organization, there have been some examples where organizations assisted migrant workers to help improve their working conditions. In 1972, the Eastern Farm Workers Association (EFWA) was established by a group of local civic groups in Suffolk County who were concerned that not enough was being done to advance the direct services or poverty programs aimed to assist the migrant farmworkers. Located in Bellport, the EFWA is a free and voluntary organization composed of seasonal farm laborers, low- and middle-income workers in a variety of occupations and those who are unemployed or underemployed. Founders of the group included farmworkers and those with experience in public service and the civil rights movement. For a voluntary monthly contribution of sixty-two cents, members are provided with a comprehensive benefits plan, which includes emergency food and clothing, preventative medical care, legal assistance and a literacy campaign.[283] The association focuses on obtaining the rights and benefits for their best interest and have held fundraisers and musical concerts to help the migrant cause.[284]

A key objective of the EFWA had always been to visit labor camps throughout the area offering support, and it continues to do so today. Most notably, the EFWA assisted in what was touted as one of the first organized informational picketing actions that involved migrant farmworkers on Long Island.[285] On December 4, 1972, a group of workers at the I.M. Young potato processing plant in Riverhead walked off the job and began an informational picketing action to alert the public that they were not being paid because the growers were holding back the sale of potatoes to drive up costs. The action was led by one of the workers at the plant, Aurestus Harris, EFWA leader Eugenio Perente, a former associate of Cesar Chavez, and Arthur Josh Herron. Known as "Big Arthur," Herron was a former crew leader who later served as interim president of the EFWA and spent much of his life advocating for farmworkers. When the workers were wrongfully evicted from the I.M Young labor camp, Herron, who was a very large man, used his bare hands to remove boards blocking the entrance.[286]

A large part of the group's success can also be attributed to its grassroots organizing led by people like Clifford Cody. Born in Augusta, Georgia, Cody came to Long Island in 1959 and spent time in a labor camp in Riverhead working at various farms and potato graders. Over the years, Cody worked in sanitation and several other occupations. However, he always remained active in assisting migrant workers, became a lead organizer for the EFWA and was instrumental in the informational picketing action at the I.M. Young plant. The EFWA is unique in that it was the first to provide an inclusive environment where migrant farmworkers received not only benefits and assistance but also the respect and dignity of being part of a fraternal organization that focuses on the collective interests of its members.

Lastly, the efforts of labor unions who represented the workers at the processing plants in the agriculture and duck industries were also laudable. In 1955, the Amalgamated Meat Cutters and Butcher Workers of North America Union successfully negotiated a three-year contract for 180 workers at the Celic Duck Processing Plant in Riverhead.[287] The contract provided hourly wage increases, more paid time off for the workers and a guaranteed four months of work during the seasonal operation. The contract was not achieved without a struggle as the company continued its operations despite the round-the-clock picketing by the workers. However, the company agreed to settle on the contract because many of its clients refused to accept its products for fear of union reprisals.

In 1974, the United Brotherhood of Industrial Workers Local 424 negotiated the first labor contract in New York State on behalf of 125 migrant workers at A&P potato packinghouses in Northville, Riverhead and Water Mill.[288] In addition to securing quality medical benefits, the three-year contract provided a guaranteed pay rate of $2.45 per hour, with $0.10 increases for each year of the contract.

The staunch efforts of these good-hearted individuals, along with various social and religious organizations referenced in this chapter, served as a true beacon of hope and helped combat the abuse and misery suffered by farmworkers trapped in the migratory labor system in Suffolk County.

The Cost of Inaction

In the mid-1950s, Long Island reporter Ruth Schier wrote extensively on the problems faced by Suffolk County from the migratory labor system.[289] In describing the many different viewpoints of migrant workers at the time, Schier stated, "The southern migrant worker is America's most irresponsible, most hard working, most improvident, most victimized, most destructive, most exploited, most unresponsive, most disenfranchised citizen, according to your point of view. Of all the people who deal with the migrant worker none can really figure him out. Some curse him, some like him, some exploit him, some defend him. The migrant turns his face to all."[290]

The differing opinions of the migrant workers thwarted any real possibility of forming a general consensus on how to deal with the problem. As a result, there was no sufficient public outcry, and county officials were never truly compelled to resolve the gradually worsening migratory labor system. Such governmental inertia came at a steep price, which was measured not only by the human suffering at the labor camps but also the Suffolk County economy. Schier estimated that the strains placed on local law enforcement and the courts, the health care system, social services and housing ranged between $3 and $4 million per year.[291] Despite these figures, which surely increased over the years, the county remained indifferent to the problem.

The abysmal and worsening conditions at the labor camps also placed local law enforcement and first responders, who were already operating with limited resources, in greater danger than their professions already entailed. Joseph Grattan, retired chief and thirty-nine-year member of the Riverhead Police Department, recalled the struggles of responding to calls for help at many of the labor camps in the area. "In those days," he stated, "we only had 4 to 5 officers on patrol each by ourselves. There were no radios or cell phones. We had call boxes at various street locations. If there was trouble at a camp, you had three options; find a call box to get help, talk your way out of trouble or fight your way out of trouble."[292]

The altercation at the Cutchogue labor camp in 1954 between state troopers and Jesse Morgan left Morgan badly injured but placed all parties at risk of injury. In 1970, several officers responded to reports of shots fired at the Cutchogue camp. When they arrived, they found at least one automatic weapon and arrested four individuals. In 1975, three Southampton police officers were injured while responding to a reported melee at the Baldwin labor camp in Bridgehampton when their car slid off the rain-slick road and crashed into a bridge abutment.[293] These are but a few examples of the

The Central Suffolk Hospital in Riverhead, New York. The hospital has been treating patients since it first opened in 1951. *Courtesy of Leslie Mashmann.*

added threats faced by local police who were tasked with maintaining law and order at and around the labor camps.

Local fire firefighters and other health care professionals who responded to calamitous situations at the labor camps were also affected. The 1961 fire at the Cutchogue labor camp required 120 firefighters from nearby towns to ultimately extinguish. For most labor camps, proper water pressure was not available, which further added to the risk. Health care professionals also shouldered the burden, particularly in the wake of mass casualties. Leslie Mashmann, a retired nurse who worked at Central Suffolk Hospital in Riverhead, explained the traumatizing encounters when bodies that were still burning from a fire were rushed into the emergency room.[294] Clearly, the wretched conditions of the labor camps placed an additional and often dangerous burden on all first responders in the area.

Suffolk County officials were always aware of the problem and for years had debated how to address it. In 1953, a joint committee on migratory labor held a series of public hearings at the Riverhead High School auditorium to address the conditions at the migrant labor camps.[295] Specifically, residents complained about the decrepit and unsanitary housing at the camps, along with fears of disease and crime. Minna F. Kassner, president of the Consumers League of New York for Fair Labor Standards, argued for the creation of a migrant farm labor division in the Department of Labor. "The problem of migrants is a complex one which cuts across the functions of many agencies and departments of government," she said. "Coordination is not enough; there must be power as well as responsibility to the plan and carry out an all-over program." Ultimately, the committee recommended the strict enforcement of the sanitary code at the labor camps, but no other strategy to truly remedy the problem was developed.

In 1958, Herbert Hill, labor secretary of the NAACP, filed a complaint with Governor Harriman, alleging that the New York Department of Labor was failing to help migrant workers who were trapped in a "vicious system of economic exploitation."[296] Hill also charged that the Department of Health is "derelict in its responsibility to secure decent living facilities for migratory farm workers." Three years later, federal and state agencies announced that a subcommittee, led by U.S. representative for New York Herbert Zelenko, was formed to investigate a series of allegations of abuse at migrant labor camps throughout New York and New Jersey.[297] A report detailing the findings by the committee was submitted to U.S. Attorney Robert F. Kennedy.[298] Unfortunately, no significant action was taken.

H. Lee Dennison served as the first county executive of Suffolk County, with a tenure that spanned from 1960 to 1972.[299] He was known for several accomplishments, including the conversion of Suffolk from a rural county to a major suburban enclave, and was once described as the man who "dragged Suffolk County into modern times." Dennison was also responsible for overseeing the construction of major highways and public buildings, the growth of the county's community college, the police district and a major parkland acquisition preservation project. Lee Koppelman served in the Dennison administration as the director of the Suffolk County Planning Department from 1960 to 1988. Now in retirement, Koppelman reflected on his work with Dennison, whom he described as a no-nonsense leader who "called it like he saw it" and a man who "refused to cater to anyone."[300]

Koppelman also explained that Dennison vigorously opposed the migratory labor system and, in particular, the exploitation of the farmworkers by crew leaders. In 1968, Dennison spoke before the newly formed Seasonal Farm Labor Commission and openly advocated for an end to the migrant labor system in Suffolk County.[301] During his speech, he warned that if the migrant labor system was not abolished, the county would continue to pay the price for bad publicity, and residents would suffer from higher taxes and increased costs to the county's health and welfare systems. He referred to the airing of the documentary *What Harvest for the Reaper?* and stated that the problem had become "a matter of national advertising that I don't really care for." Two years later, Dennison issued a scathing public statement deriding the health conditions at some of the migrant labor camps, which were cited for numerous violations. He wrote, "The only way this County Executive knows to correct such situations is to eliminate the importation of migrant labor and the camps. Period."[302]

Ultimately, Dennison's public disdain for the migratory labor system remained largely rhetorical. After all, he was an elected official in a rural county known for its large agricultural output and was facing a very powerful agricultural industry that was unafraid to wield its power.[303] Any new proposals to improve upon the system, and certainly ones that would have been unduly burdensome to the growers, were met with fierce resistance from his constituents. Thus while Dennison and other county officials publicly professed a strong desire to bring about much-needed reforms, they lacked the support of their constituents and ultimately the political will to implement any real change. By the early 1970s, Dennison's crusade against the broken system appeared to have waned, and he meekly stated, "The migrant situation is gradually handling itself."[304]

Unfortunately, the local government's failure to address the migratory labor problem adversely affected the lives of many migrant farmworkers who were trapped in the system. This inaction had not only a limiting effect on the advocacy efforts referenced throughout this chapter, but it also had dangerous effects on the first responders of the area and was very costly to the local economy each year. Collectively, this was the cost of the county's inaction toward the migratory labor system.

SETTLEMENT IN RIVERHEAD

INTRODUCTION

The town of Riverhead is Long Island's easternmost municipal city. It rests at the mouth of the Peconic River where the North and South Forks split. To the east of Riverhead lie various hamlets and much smaller towns all the way to Orient on the North Fork and extending to Montauk on the South Fork. By 1960, the towns of Riverhead and nearby Southold accounted for more than 50 percent of the total migrant workers in Suffolk County.[305] When the other townships east of Riverhead were factored in, they collectively accounted for 60 percent of the total labor camps at that time and 70 percent of the total migrant workforce countywide. Given Riverhead's proximity, many of the migrant workers in Suffolk County who chose to leave the migrant stream and settle on Long Island likely did so there.

Suffolk County was also known as one of the world's largest suppliers of ducks for consumption. In many ways, the duck and agricultural industries ran similar courses. They both were known to be among the largest suppliers in their respective industries and both required large labor forces to operate efficiently. However, by the mid-1960s, the duck industry was winding down dramatically and for sharply different reasons, which had a dramatic impact on the community. This section explores the effects on the lives of migrant workers who settled in Riverhead, along with the impact on the community from the fall of the Long Island duck industry.

THE RISE AND FALL OF THE
LONG ISLAND DUCK INDUSTRY

The first reference to raising ducks on Long Island dates to 1824, when William Corbett published a book titled *Cottage Economy*. However, raising ducks for consumption as a full-time industry probably did not begin on Long Island until about 1880–85. Globally, the duck industry produced three classes of ducks: the meat class, the egg class and the ornamental class. Ducks in the United States were used almost exclusively for meat. The breeds of duck in the meat class included Muscovy, Rouen, Aylesbury, Cayuga and Pekin (later changed to Peking). The peak of the Long Island duck industry occurred between the 1930s and the 1950s.[306] Throughout that time, nearly one hundred duck farms operated on Long Island and produced between six and eight million ducks per year.

In 1929, Hollis V. Warner purchased a duck farm from Dennis G. Homan. The twenty-acre property had a water frontage to the Peconic River in the eastern section of Riverhead.[307] Over the years, Warner, who was a Cornell University graduate, would go on to eventually amass hundreds of acres of land, and his ranch became the largest supplier of ducks in the world, with an estimated output of more than five hundred thousand ducks annually. In the mid-1940s, Warner began to employ more workers to assist with his lucrative business, along with the harvesting of some crops he grew on his sprawling ranch.[308]

Tending to the upkeep of millions of ducks was no easy task. By day, the ducks were allowed to roam freely on the grounds and in local ponds, bays and streams. To feed the ducks, Warner constructed a three-mile-long narrow railway track that was traversed by a vehicle used to distribute a protein-rich meal composed of wheat, corn and flour. During the evenings, the ducks were housed in approximately seventy buildings throughout the ranch, which required constant cleaning and maintenance. Some of these buildings were more than four hundred feet long and served as sheds, or brooders. Workers also collected and cultivated the eggs and hatchlings, assisted in the slaughtering process and prepared the birds for delivery to nearby processing plants to be frozen and eventually shipped to consumers. Some of the workers were pickers, whose sole job was to pluck the feathers off the slaughtered ducks. This was a lucrative part of Warner's business, as six ducks yielded a pound of feathers with a value of nearly one dollar.

Hollis Warner and other business leaders went to great lengths to promote the duck industry. In 1948, local duck farmers took part in the Long Island

The Big Duck on Flanders Road in Flanders, New York. Erected in 1931, the twenty-foot-tall, thirty-foot-long and fifteen-foot-wide building shaped like a Pekin duck remains as a token of the once thriving Long Island duck industry. *Courtesy of Mark Torres.*

Poultry Parade, where they hosted a large group of food experts from around the world to promote their thriving $11 million per year business.[309] They proudly promoted the Big Duck, a twenty-foot-tall, thirty-foot-long and fifteen-foot-wide building shaped like a Pekin duck. First erected in 1931, the Big Duck was then, and remains today, a token of the duck industry.

Five years later, a large group of duck farmers formed the Riverhead Duck Processing Cooperative. The cooperative invested $500,000 to construct a state-of-the-art processing plant on Elton Street in Riverhead. The plant had an assembly line where the ducks were slaughtered, plucked, packaged and then sent to blast freeze rooms with temperatures at sixty degrees below zero, before being stored or prepared for shipment.[310] Within a few years, the cooperative was able to process more than fifty-three million pounds of duck per year.

By 1960, a group of area duck farmers had formed the Long Island Duck Farmer's Cooperative to address their collective interests. The group set prices, centralized processing and continued with its widespread promotional advertisements.

Over the years, New York State placed more stringent environmental regulations on the duck industry to prevent the pollution of Long Island's bays and inlets. This forced duck farmers to invest heavily in wastewater treatment plants and to make extensive changes in operations. For most in the industry, these new measures proved to be very costly. As a result, many went out of business, and the total number of duck farms dwindled. By the mid-1960s, there were forty-four farms remaining, and by 1974, there were just twenty-seven farms remaining on Long Island producing seven million ducks per year. Today, the Crescent Duck Farm on Hubbard Avenue in Aquebogue is one of the last duck farms remaining of this once thriving industry.

ENVIRONMENTAL IMPACTS

Before the implementation of environmental protections, the duck industry was largely underregulated. It would not be clearly known until later how destructive the industry was on both the environment and other industries. In his role as the director of the Suffolk County Planning Department, Lee Koppelman explained that the duck industry was among the worst polluters. "In the early days," stated Koppelman, "the workers would cut up the ducks and throw the entrails right into the river." The former Riverhead chief of police Joseph Grattan recalled how children used to slide down mountains of duck excrement at various farms.

Over time, the duck industry was viewed negatively. This shift began when the public and officials in other industries realized the serious threats it posed to the environment and habitats. As a result, the number of pollution complaints grew exponentially. In 1951, a report compiled by the Woods Hole Oceanographic Institution showed that duck waste was prohibiting proper water flow necessary to sustain a healthy production of oysters. This drew great ire from shellfish industry officials, who bitterly complained about a decline in oysters in the Great South Bay.[311] Similar studies were scheduled to determine the extent of the damage in the Peconic Bay, Flanders Bay and other key waterways.[312]

With the polluting effects becoming more apparent, New York was compelled to act. In 1954, the Department of Health ordered all duck farms to construct and use waste disposal facilities. Once implemented, there were immediate signs of improvement in places like the Moriches inlet, which serves as a filter for the Great South Bay, and fisherman reported phenomenal growth of marine wildlife, including oysters.[313]

County health inspectors also began to enforce the health laws more rigorously. In 1956, four duck farmers from Calverton and Riverhead were charged with polluting the Peconic Bay.[314] Two years later, the New York attorney general brought charges against the Griffin and Havens Duck Farm in Flanders and the Gallo Duck Farm in East Patchogue for violating the public health law by polluting the Peconic River and the Great South Bay.[315] The complaint alleged that both farms were draining duck waste into these critical waterways and causing extensive damage. The defendants were issued fines, which accumulated each day until they rectified their operations. In November 1963, several duck farm owners were charged with contaminating the waterways of Brookhaven, Riverhead and Southold townships.[316] The complaint alleged numerous violations of the public health law for pollution of state waterways. Fines for these violations included an initial $500 and then $100 each day until the violations were remedied.

Calls for change to the duck industry continued. During a 1966 conference in Patchogue, Senator Robert F. Kennedy issued a dire warning about how the water pollution in the Moriches and the Great South Bay would greatly injure the shellfish industry and Long Island's beaches and waterways and would have an adverse impact on the county's economy.[317] He stated, "Unfortunately, the wastes produced from these duck farms are carried into streams, tide and seepage into these bays. If the water circulation in the bays is poor, the area banned to shellfish harvesters is increased. And if these wastes are not limited, all of the Moriches and Great South Bays may be placed off limits to shell fisherman."

Over the years, efforts to curb the pollution intensified. In 1972, the state health department issued a ninety-day deadline to twenty-one Suffolk County duck farms to clean up the sewage created on their properties or face the loss of their permits, which would eventually shutter their operations. If they were forced to close, they would have been compelled to remove all of the existing duck waste, which would have been even more costly.[318] In connection with this order, the department closed four hundred acres of shellfishing waters in Flanders Bay. The strict enforcement of the environmental laws continued and, due to increasing costs, essentially led to the demise of the duck industry.

Over time, studies were conducted to understand the adverse environmental impacts caused by the duck industry. In 2009, the U.S. Army Corps of Engineers, in partnership with the Suffolk County Department of Planning, conducted a comprehensive historical study of the waste produced at the thirty-four remaining farms in Suffolk County in 1968.[319] The data had shown that these farms, which raised seven million ducks in that year, created seventy tons of solids per day. This duck waste would seep into the local estuaries, creating blankets of sludge and leaving harmful organic decomposing matter that adversely affected wildlife and left strong foul odors. The volume of this sludge was significant. A survey of Moriches Bay was taken in 1968 and showed that an estimated 7.3 million cubic yards of sludge was deposited. The study also focused on the release of harmful compounds like nitrate, which depletes available oxygen in the water and kills fish. Since nitrate is highly mobile, it also can leach downward through the soil and into groundwater.

Unlike with the migrant labor camps, the duck industry caused severe environmental and economic impacts that were impossible to ignore. As a result, there was a significant public and commercial outcry that compelled the government to act by increasing regulations, which ultimately led to the downfall of the industry. However, as it will be shown, the demise of the duck industry, and specifically the closure of the Hollis Warner duck farm, played a significant role in the housing crisis in the town of Riverhead.

The Riverhead Housing Problem

Before 1968, Riverhead was one of the few townships on Long Island that lacked a housing code. This had a devastating impact on the town and led to the growth of several distinct neighborhoods that were deemed to be "rural slums." The first of these areas was located on the sprawling Hollis Warner duck ranch, which was bounded by Hubbard Avenue to the north, Riverside Drive to the east and the Peconic River to the south.

By the late 1950s, many duck farmers were struggling to meet the demands of increased environmental regulations and began to wind down their businesses. During this time, Hollis Warner converted many of the buildings that he used to house ducks on his property into crude living spaces and rented them to migrant workers. These structures lacked heat, running water and bathroom facilities. Warner had already been renting many of the shacks on his property to impoverished residents of Riverhead. At the time his ranch ceased operations, there were approximately five hundred people residing on the property who were living in squalor and virtually stranded. Without any restrictions to prevent Warner from converting these structures into housing units, the Town of Riverhead essentially encouraged the growth of this poverty-stricken area.

In 1959, two reporters investigated the conditions of the ranch and described the setting as follows:

> *Here inside the woods* [on the Hollis Warner duck farm]…*is a community of "new" homes that have mushroomed in the last few years. It's hometown for several hundred Negro men, woman and children. But "across the bridge" as this new colony is called, has no paved roads, sidewalks, or street lighting. It has no water system, sewer system, or shopping center….* *The houses, laid out in rows and numbered, are constructed of wallboard panels and corrugated metal set on a few cement blocks. None of the 30 houses in the woods have inside tubs, toilets, or showers. In fact, the only bathroom facilities in the entire colony consist of rows of outhouses stuck in the backyards.*[320]

On one side of the Warner property, a string of shanty homes had sprung up on what was called Main Street. Those who resided on this portion of the property paid twelve dollars per week to live in these shacks, along with an additional two dollars for a refrigerator. The weekly cost for a five-room cabin was fifteen dollars. One migrant worker, who was twelve years old when she came to Long Island from North Carolina, explained that Hollis Warner collected the rent himself. She stated, "He never gives you a receipt neither. And if you miss payments, he'll put a lock on your door and you can't get your stuff. He also sells food to us because we can't get into town very often. I don't think the meat he sells is good and he sells us stale bread he gets in town cheap. If you're short on money he'll loan you that too, but you pay plenty." She added, "Something should be done about this place. My mother's been sick most of the time here. You can't keep warm in the winter unless you hang around the stove."

The other side of the Warner property was accessible by crossing a pedestrian bridge adorned with a sign that read "Warning: Bridges Unsafe." Those who visited this area could not escape the putrid stench from the open garbage dump in the nearby woods. A large number of brooders, feeding pens and assorted farm buildings that were used for many years

Piles of duck manure lined up outside a duck brooder house on R.A. Tuthill's Farm, Center Moriches, 1920. *Courtesy of the National Archives, No. 17-P-16-125.*

to house the ducks on the sprawling ranch were converted into eight-by-seven-foot residential apartments. Those who lived in the higher floors of these structures had to climb rickety stairs to gain entry, and the foul odor of duck emanated throughout each building. A mother with four children who lived in one of these apartments paid sixty dollars per month to rent one of these apartments, plus extra fees for a refrigerator, stove and fuel. "The worst thing about this place," she stated, "is fighting the roaches and bedbugs. They're awful."

In the spring of 1964, the Long Island chapter of the Congress on Racial Equality (CORE), under the leadership of Lincoln Lynch, collaborated with filmmaker David Hoffman to produce a fifteen-minute documentary titled *Got to Move*. The film chronicles the squalid conditions of the Hollis Warner duck ranch.[321] In the film, one resident on the ranch states, "This is nowhere for a dog to live....It wasn't even good enough for ducks—they moved them out." When asked about the film, Lynch stated, "We're trying to show how things actually exist in Riverhead. These people live there. They want better homes but can't get them because of discrimination and bigotry."

Later that year, Delores Quintyne of CORE visited the duck ranch with representatives of the League of Woman Voters to register residents to vote. On one occasion, Lynch and other CORE officials established a makeshift office inside one of the shacks on the ranch and engaged in

This page: A duck brooder house on R.A. Tuthill's Farm, Center Moriches, 1920. This type of building was common on most duck farms on Long Island, including the Hollis Warner duck ranch. When the industry was winding down, Mr. Warner converted duck brooders on his property into apartments without heating or plumbing, which he rented to impoverished laborers. *Courtesy of the National Archives, No. 17-P-16-115.*

several demonstrations to protest against the living conditions. County officials were outraged, and when the officials attempted to evict them, Lynch and the others barricaded themselves inside the shack. After a brief standoff, they vacated the premises, and Lynch was arrested for trespassing. Later, Lynch and two other CORE members were arrested for dumping a

A laborer shoveling duck feed from a horse-drawn food wagon on R.A. Tuthill's Farm, Center Moriches, 1920. Hollis Warner constructed a three-mile-long narrow railway track on his sprawling ranch that was traversed by a vehicle used to distribute a protein-rich meal to the ducks. *Courtesy of the National Archives, No. 17-P-16-107.*

truckload of garbage from the Warner property near the Riverhead Town Hall to protest the conditions at the farm.[322] Due to these actions, Lynch and two of his deputies were barred from participating in a charity event where local groups collected and distributed clothing, furniture, shoes and toys to families at the ranch.[323]

During the same period, the number of farmworkers who left the migrant stream and settled in Riverhead and other areas continued to increase. According to the Suffolk County Labor Department, in 1964, there were approximately 1,000 seasonal farmworkers who settled in the county, including Riverhead.[324] By 1971, that number rose to about 1,600.[325] One migrant worker stated, "Why did I stay? Because I hope to make some money. You can't make money on the season no more."[326]

Most of the migrant workers who settled in Riverhead were relegated to various slum-like neighborhoods in the city limits. Without a housing code, many of these families were allowed to use or construct makeshift structures that were not fireproofed and lacked heating and plumbing. Over time, these neighborhoods became known as the Bottoms. Social justice groups who visited these areas described them as "shantytowns" and "poverty in its rawest form."[327] Betty Coles, from a Long Island–based charity group, visited the homes and found two children with ringworm and a family of six in one room huddled around a wood-burning stove only eighteen inches from a

Delores Quintyne (*far right, wearing glasses*) of the Congress of Racial Equality (CORE) visits the Hollis Warner duck ranch in 1964 to assist migrant workers with voter registration. *Courtesy of The Delores Quintyne Collection.*

bed. She also met with a fifteen-year-old mother with a child suffering from malnutrition sharing a six-by-six-foot living space with the child's father and another couple, multiple dwellings with defective plumbing and a father of seven children who was bedridden and unable to work after a recent surgery.

One of these slum-like neighborhoods was an area bounded by Roanoke Avenue, Telephone Street and Griffing Avenue and only blocks away from the Riverhead High School and the local courthouse. This neighborhood consisted of more than one hundred residents who lived in about forty dilapidated shacks. These structures lacked heating and plumbing and were beleaguered by faulty drainage, which often left the area flooded after heavy rains.[328] One resident testified that they were forced to get their drinking water from a single pipe and there were only three toilets, all of which were outside.[329] William Leonard was once the town supervisor of Riverhead and had been accused of making racially insensitive public comments regarding the residents of these neighborhoods. He explained the origin of the name, stating, "We called it the Bottom of the world because everybody that dropped off the tailboard of the migrant truck seemed to sift down there

Lincoln Lynch, the Long Island chair of the Congress of Racial Equality (CORE), being arrested in 1964 for trespassing after protesting the living conditions of the migrant workers at the Hollis Warner duck ranch in Riverhead, New York. *Courtesy of Newsday LLC.*

eventually."[330] Sadly, it was the town's ineffective and indifferent leadership, largely during Leonard's tenure, that enabled the formation of these neighborhoods.

Another one of these poverty-stricken neighborhoods in the city of Riverhead was at the intersection of Horton Avenue, Osborne Avenue and Middle Road.[331] Here, about 150 people resided in approximately fifty rundown homes surrounded by farmland area.[332] Other neighborhoods were located off Hubbard Avenue between Poor Lane and Edgar Avenue and an area known as the Greens, which was an abandoned golf course in western Riverhead.[333]

In 1954, Dr. Philip J. Rafle, the Suffolk County health commissioner, inspected the extreme slum conditions at nearly all of the units in these neighborhoods.[334] To alleviate the unsanitary conditions, Rafle urged the implementation of a housing code and recommended that the town extend the water and sewer lines into that area, but his recommendations were not

This page: An abandoned home and an abandoned shack in the former poverty-stricken area known as the Bottoms in Riverhead, New York. *Courtesy of Leslie Mashmann.*

Telephone Street in Riverhead, New York. The overgrown vegetation on the right was once part of the Bottoms, which was occupied by impoverished laborers who inhabited rundown shacks and shanties. *Courtesy of Leslie Mashmann.*

An abandoned shack in Riverhead, New York. *Courtesy of Leslie Mashmann.*

carried out. Even though town supervisor William Leonard described the Bottoms as a "disgrace," he remained opposed to the creation of a public housing code, which could have alleviated the problem. Instead, Leonard traded blame with other county officials while those who resided in these areas continued to languish. Albert Seay, president of the Eastern Long Island branch of the NAACP, criticized the acute housing shortage that developed after the postwar boom in Suffolk County. He added, "As long as anything can be built and called housing, I think the rural slums will spread."[335]

After the horrific deaths of young children in these neighborhoods in 1959, the Town of Riverhead initiated a "slum-clearance" drive to raise funds to establish alternate housing. Unfortunately, after only seven months, the town board cut all funding for the drive, due to a reported lack of public support. Two years later, Sidney Beckwith, the Suffolk County Health Department sanitarian, argued that more should be done to address the housing problem.[336] "It is a little ridiculous," commented Beckwith, "that we have construction codes for migrant camps in Riverhead, but all around them people can put up shacks."

In 1964, Hyman Bookbinder, the executive director of President Lyndon B. Johnson's antipoverty program, toured these neighborhoods in Riverhead. He greeted children on the dusty, unpaved roads and viewed the dilapidated clapboard shanties, many of which had missing windows and doors. Bookbinder stated that "some of the houses I've seen are as bad as I've seen, and I've spent some time in Harlem and Appalachia." He added, "I find a feeling of despair among these people. I don't find much hope. Nobody can look at these living conditions and be indifferent." Bookbinder notified local officials that the federal government would fund up to 90 percent of the cost to improve the area. Still, no action was taken.

One year later, plans for a new development to be constructed off Doctor's Path, north of Northville Turnpike in Riverhead, was announced.[337] The project, which was to be funded by private investors, sought to build nearly eighty rental units and sixty-five single-family homes. Civil rights groups and local leaders expressed a deep concern that the high rental fees for homes in the development would make welfare assistance necessary for the low-income families who were expected to live there, thus turning the development into what was called a "negro ghetto." County executive Dennison stated, "I'm not wholly in support of this type of segregated housing, but it's better than nothing. This is kind of a key."

In an effort to alleviate the problem, the Suffolk County Opportunity Council sponsored a home construction program for impoverished families to construct their own homes.[338] James Smith, a farm laborer and handyman, along with seven other migrant workers, enrolled in the program. "I never thought I could own a home like this," stated Smith. As an added benefit, home equity accumulated based on the number of labor hours they put into building the homes. For the 1,500 hours of labor Mr. Smith worked, he earned $7,000 in home equity. Unfortunately, such projects were limited in scope and did not make a significant impact to the town's self-inflicted housing crisis.

After many years of woeful inaction, the Town of Riverhead finally adopted a new housing code in 1968, which was aimed at improving the poor housing conditions in the city and preventing the creation of future problems.[339] The ordinance was modeled after the New York State code and applied only to rental homes and multiple-family homes. However, homes where the owner also resided were exempt. The new code set responsibilities for tenants and provided for their eviction if they failed to "maintain standards of neatness and cleanliness in rented housing." It also allowed for the reduction of rental rates by court order if landlords failed to provide heat, plumbing, maintenance and hot water. Since the new code covered only about 50 percent of the homes in Riverhead, it was criticized for being too narrow. Nevertheless, Town Supervisor Robert Vojvoda argued that "it was better than nothing."

As Riverhead grappled with its housing crisis, the county set its sights much sooner on the wretched conditions at the Hollis Warner duck ranch, which had evolved into the town's most poverty-stricken area. In 1962, the Suffolk Board of Supervisors approved a $4 million wetlands acquisition project.[340] Under the plan, which was spearheaded by county executive Lee Dennison, New York State paid $3 million, and Suffolk County paid the remaining portion.

One year later, Suffolk County purchased 462 acres of the former Hollis Warner duck ranch for an estimated $500,000. Once acquired, the county implemented costly efforts to clear out the streams, creeks and soil that had long been polluted by duck waste. Later that year, the township demolished some of the shanty homes on the ranch.[341] However, the town still grappled with where to relocate the remaining residents who were still living in the dilapidated homes on the ranch. Sidney Beckwith was appointed by Lee Dennison to serve as the coordinating agent for the establishment of low-cost rental units throughout the county.[342] Eventually, some residents were relocated to more suitable housing in the towns of Bellport and Huntington. The county also hired a New York City firm to further assist with the relocation project.[343] By 1964, all of the residents were relocated, and the town razed the remaining shanty homes on the ranch.[344] Today, a large portion of the site that was once this infamous Hollis Warner duck ranch is now the publicly accessible Indian Island County Park with an adjoining golf course. There are no discernible remnants of the duck ranch and ensuing poverty-stricken area that existed for nearly half a century.

After years of futility, Suffolk County finally resolved the housing crisis at the Hollis Warner duck farm. In finally adopting a housing code in 1968, Riverhead also began to address the so-called rural slums. Unfortunately, the long-delayed response in addressing the housing problems in all of these locations had a dramatic impact on the lives of those who resided there and adversely affected the Riverhead community for many years to come.

DEATH IN RIVERHEAD

The lack of a housing code in Riverhead led to poverty-stricken neighborhoods that arose in the city limits and at the Hollis Warner duck ranch. The impoverished families, many of whom were migrant laborers, were forced to fend for themselves by constructing and using makeshift structures as their domiciles. These homes were poorly built without heating or plumbing, lacked proper insulation and were not fireproofed. As a result, in a desperate attempt to provide warmth during cold weather, the occupants used kerosene heaters or stoves, which far too often had deadly consequences.

On October 25, 1952, Mark McCain, a forty-three-year-old laborer and army air force veteran, and his wife perished in a blaze that quickly consumed their one-room shack on the Hollis Warner duck ranch.[345] Their charred bodies were discovered by firefighters who battled the fire. In a horrific span of eleven days in 1959, eight people, including young children, perished in various fires at slum-like shacks and shanties throughout Riverhead. On January 29, Dilsia Trent, a twenty-two-year-old mother and wife of Earl Trent, a migrant laborer, was critically injured while trying to save her children from a fire that erupted in their twelve-by-twelve-foot shanty home on Horton Avenue in Riverhead.[346] According to the police, Mrs. Trent lit a kerosene space heater to warm up the area for her children. However, she accidentally dropped the match, which ignited a rug that was saturated with kerosene spillage, setting off the blaze.[347] As she attempted to remove the flaming rug through a small door in the room, the kerosene heater fell over and intensified the flames. She then tried to stand the eighty-pound heater up, but when she did, kerosene poured onto her clothing, effectively turning her into a human torch. As the flames intensified, Mrs. Trent was forced to abandon her children, Albert (three), Catherine (one) and Earl Jr. 9 (two weeks) inside the burning home to desperately extinguish her flaming body by rolling around on the muddied ground outside. All three children perished in the fire, and Mrs. Trent, who suffered burns on over 80 percent of her body, died one week later. Firefighters arrived on the scene within minutes and later stated, "It would have been impossible to reach the kids. The place was a mass of flames."

Days later, a twenty-seven-year-old migrant laborer named Abraham Miles was found burned to death at the foot of his bed in a cement block home in Riverhead from a fire caused by a faulty kerosene space heater. Miles had collapsed by the bed after he attempted to escape. That same day, the bodies of Shirley Ann Wright (two), Jo Ann Green (sixteen months) and infant child Darlene Green were pulled from a burning twenty-by-twenty-foot shanty on Pleasant Avenue in Riverhead. A faulty kerosene heater was once again blamed for the fire. Both of the older children were killed by either asphyxiation or carbon monoxide poisoning, and the infant child was rushed to the hospital in critical condition.[348] Police believe that she miraculously survived because of an air pocket in her bassinet. One week later, thirty-three-year-old Nathanial Cobb was killed when a fire erupted in his nine-by-ten-foot shack that he rented at the Hollis Warner duck ranch.[349] Cobb's charred remains were found by two fellow migrant workers, who stated that he had no chance of escape. Several months later, a total of three more lives were claimed by fire, including Herman Howard, who died when a two-burner kerosene stove he was using exploded, causing a fire to immediately engulf the one-room shanty he inhabited.[350]

In response to this rash of fires, the NAACP demanded that the Town of Riverhead "bend every effort" to enforce existing laws and adopt new ones. It also demanded that town supervisor William J. Leonard repudiate racially insensitive remarks he had made in the wake of one fire when he stated, "No state or person should go socialistic and I'm not going to ask the taxpayers for money for people who are too ignorant to help themselves." Leonard attempted to defend his comments by adding that he did not single out any one particular race.

On April 25, 1963, fifteen-month-old Joseph W. Jones and his three-month-old sister, Elizabeth, burned to death when a fire swept through their twenty-by-twenty-foot slum shack at the Hollis Warner duck ranch.[351] Their eight-year-old sister, Darrell, barely escaped the blaze alive. At the time the tragedy occurred, their father had been working for a landscaper and their mother was visiting a neighbor's house a mere fifty feet away. Despite these deadly fires, Riverhead supervisor William Leonard remained indifferent and stated, "Just because there is a fire in a slum, everyone thinks we should rush out and pass a law. I have no plans to take any action."

In response to these fires, Marion Hoag, editor of the *Suffolk County News*, penned a scathing editorial in 1963 condemning the community's inaction. Hoag stated, "So two babies burned in a shanty in Riverhead. Oh, well. They were colored babies and their mother couldn't love them as much as white mothers love their children. It is their fault that they live in the slums that they have down there....How can we call ourselves Christians and tolerate a condition which allows, to say nothing of, forces, other human beings to live in squalor?"[352] Hoag demanded action, stating, "Every one of us should use any influence we have to wipe out this blot."

Lastly, the death of Spanish Magee acutely captures the plight of one migrant worker who left the migrant stream and remained in Riverhead. Born in 1929 in Crawford, Mississippi, Magee joined the East Coast migrant stream at a young age. By the 1950s, he was working in dusty warehouses in Riverhead, sorting and bagging potatoes and loading trucks. The sharp decline of the potato industry ultimately left Magee without a job and homeless.

Spanish Magee was described as a large but gentle man. Locals regularly saw him walking through town wearing a long black overcoat and accompanied by his two dogs, Bimbo, a hound, and a large black mutt named Midnight. "He loved those dogs like they were his children," stated one friend. "They always got fed before he did." Magee never spoke much but was generally known to be a proud man who rarely accepted handouts, and when he did, he would always say, "Bless you, sweetheart." Since he was homeless, Magee slept with his dogs in doorways, abandoned farmhouses, chicken coops and any other place he could lie down and spread out his few belongings.[353]

During the morning hours of February 14, 1982, Spanish Magee was found dead in the doorway of a shack behind an abandoned store in Riverhead, with his body being guarded by his beloved dogs. He was fifty-two years old. News of his death saddened residents in the community. To avoid having him buried in a pauper's grave, the Long Island Council of Churches purchased a plot in the Riverhead Cemetery, and the Suffolk

A shuttered building in Riverhead, New York. On December 14, 1982, a well-known migrant laborer named Spanish McGee was found dead in a small shack he inhabited behind this building. *Courtesy of Leslie Mashmann.*

The gravesite of Spanish Magee at the Riverhead Cemetery in Riverhead, New York. *Courtesy of Leslie Mashmann.*

County Department of Social Services paid for the cost of his funeral, which was held on February 27, 1982, at the nearby Tuthill Funeral Home.

Spanish Magee was a migrant worker who left the migrant stream, and other than the companionship of his dogs, he lived a life of poverty and solitude. Although his death was not caused by an act of violence, horrific fire or deadly mode of transportation, his sad ending vividly captures the struggles of most of the migrant workers who left the migrant stream in search of a better life.

Unfortunately, years of inaction and futility culminated in the horrible deaths of numerous migrant workers and impoverished residents of Riverhead, which all stemmed from the squalid living conditions in which they were forced to reside.

THE END OF AN ERA

THE DEMISE OF THE LABOR CAMPS

In 1958, there were 134 labor camps registered throughout Suffolk County. This was the peak period of the migratory labor system. Over the years, the number of camps declined sharply, and today, there are about a dozen or so remaining. Sadly, the decline of these camps did not come in the wake of humanitarian efforts, public outcry or legislative reform like it did with the duck industry. Instead, it was changes in the agricultural industry itself that led to the ultimate demise of the labor camp era.

One of the leading changes in the agricultural industry was the increased reliance on machinery for farming purposes, particularly with equipment like the potato harvester. Horace D. Wells, who served in the Suffolk County office of the U.S. Department of Agriculture, explained, "Almost everything had to be picked by hand. Some crops, like strawberries and cauliflower, don't lend themselves to machines. But the potato combine, the farmers had to go to it. The labor had not been available, and the machine can do the work of several men."[354] The result was clear: with more machines performing the work, less manpower was needed on the farms. As a result, the number of migrant workers in Suffolk County continued a steady decline over the years, and with fewer migrant workers, the need for labor camps also declined.

Nelson Hopper, a representative of the State Farm Placement Service in Rochester, New York, stated, "The migrant stream has been shrinking since

1957 mainly because of mechanization."[355] In fact, between 1960 and 1970, the national migrant population fell from 400,000 to about 200,000.[356] In New York State, the number of migrant farmworkers fell from 27,600 in 1960 to 14,400 in 1968.[357] Lastly, in Suffolk County, there was a decline from about 4,500 workers in 1960 to an estimated 1,700 by 1971.[358] Clearly, the increased use of machinery was a leading reason for the sharp decline of migrant workers and labor camps.

The steady decline of potato production was another critical change in the agricultural industry. In 1954, Suffolk County had more than 45,000 acres of farms, which produced more than 475,000 tons of potatoes.[359] By 1975, the acreage planted in potatoes had decreased to 24,300. "We've been decreasing [acreage of potatoes] for the past 20 years," stated William Sanok from the Cooperative Extension of Suffolk County.[360] By 1997, only 5,900 acres of potatoes were cultivated, producing fewer than 100,000 tons. By 2005, there were fewer than 3,000 acres planted.[361] Just ten years later, Suffolk County was dethroned as the most lucrative agricultural producer in New York State by the upstate counties of Cayuga and Wyoming.[362]

Another critical factor that led to the decline in potato production on Long Island was the strict environmental regulations implemented by the New York State Department of Environmental Conservation (DEC). In the late 1960s, the DEC placed a ban on the use of certain pesticides in Nassau and Suffolk Counties out of fear that high levels of nitrate from these chemicals were seeping into the water aquifers and polluting drinking water.[363] Since the Long Island region made up a small geographical portion of the nation's potato industry, companies had little economic incentive to develop less harmful alternative products for this area alone.

The environmental restrictions left the potato farmers at the mercy of ravenous insects like the Colorado potato beetle, which was known to completely destroy crops. In 1973, the potato beetle was blamed for an estimated loss of $1 million to the local potato crop.[364] Tom Wickham, whose family has been farming in the Cutchogue for generations, explained how armies of these beetles could be heard crunching on the crops and could even be seen crossing roads from one patch of land to another. The lack of a safe but effective pesticide to deal with these and other types of insects contributed to the adverse economic impacts faced by the growers in the area and ultimately played a significant role in the decline of potato production in the county.

Concurrently, rising land prices, driven by New York's booming population growth, incentivized many farmers to sell off their land. According to census records, there were 2,187 farmers in 1950 who cultivated 123,346 acres of potatoes in Suffolk County. By 1964, that number declined to 1,279 farmers cultivating 89,776 acres.[365] Moreover, from 1963 to 1968, vacant land in Suffolk County decreased from 68 percent to 40 percent, and a third of the farmland had gone to make homes, schools, stores and industrial parks.

The Zuhoski family had been farming in Cutchogue for nearly one hundred years before they sold their land in 1968. Joseph Zuhoski, who was working the land in those final years with his brother Edward, stated, "My father and mother worked hard to get what we had. I love farming and it's all I ever knew, but I'm getting out while the getting's good. I had my belly-full of it. The reason I quit is that you can't make any money, it's a vicious cycle."[366] Other farmers were equally willing to sell off their land once they were able to find a buyer who would pay the right price.

The acquisition of farmland continued to accelerate, and by 1971, a third of the sixty-eight thousand farms in Suffolk County were already owned by real estate speculators. "It is the loss of the pride of ownership," explained Horace D. Wells, a Suffolk County agricultural agent, as a reason for the downward trend. He further stated:

> It used to be that a grandfather would pass the farm along to the father and then he to the son. If a person intends to pass land along, they make certain that the land is kept up. But what has happened is that the urban pressures have become too great. If there is profit in agriculture, a person will continue in it rather than leaving the land. The speculation has let up a little bit, but these are hard economic times. But a lot has been lost in the last 25–30 years. The farmers are just making a living now or a little better. If they sell the farm to a speculator to pay back taxes and bills, they owe, they can retire and live on the interest without having to do the work.

Despite the large loss of farming acreage, agriculture will always remain a fixed part of Suffolk County. Horace Wells explained that the county could not afford to lose all of the farms. "There is just not enough water for homes," he stated. "On the two Forks, there is a limit on the amount of ground water. If the farms are replaced with homes and shopping centers and businesses, the rainwater will not have an opportunity to sink through the ground. It will run off on all the concrete." Despite the need to preserve some farmland, there is no doubt that the era of the great potato production in Suffolk County is gone forever. Today, the bulk of the remaining agricultural operations include nurseries, sod farms and agritainment.[367]

Louisa Hargrave planting on her vineyard in Cutchogue, New York, in 1977 while pregnant with her first child. The Hargraves are believed to have opened the first vineyard on the North Fork. *Courtesy of the Louisa Hargrave.*

The decline of the potato farms also ushered in a period of new crops. This was keenly understood for many years by John Wickham, who began to diversify his farming operations during the height of the potato industry. Wickham was among the first area growers to diversify from vegetables alone to new varieties of apples, apricots, cherries, peaches and other fruits.[368] Similarly, Martin Sidor, a third-generation farmer, diversified his operations into the production of potato chips.

John Wickham also had a strong influence on Louisa and Alex Hargrave. The Hargraves arrived in the area in 1973 and purchased land previously owned by the Zuhoski family. They had heard of Mr. Wickham's successes and sought his advice on the possibility of growing grapes for wine production. Wickham supported their interests and lent his expert farming advice to the couple. A short time later, the Hargraves opened the first vineyard in the area. Today, there are many vineyards in the region, and the North Fork has been transformed into Long Island Wine Country, which, according to its website, attracts more than one million visitors and produces five hundred thousand cases of wine each year.[369]

It took more than four decades, but all of these changes in the agricultural industry ultimately led to the decline in the demand for migrant farmworkers and the need for labor camps in Suffolk County. The labor camps that exist today are much more regulated, rendering them but a shadow of the labor camps of the past. Lee Dennison once proclaimed that the migrant labor problem would eventually take care of itself. Sadly, this declaration turned out to be true, but it did not come from reforms aimed at minimizing human suffering. Instead, it was resolved because the agricultural industry no longer required the amount of manpower that it once did.

Shameful Legacy

Throughout the twentieth century, potato and other crop production in Suffolk County was a multimillion-dollar industry. It helped feed a nation during World War II and continued as a top food producer for many years. This thriving industry required a large amount of human labor to perform essential services that local residents refused or were unable to do. Each year, migrant workers came to the area by the thousands. They were lured by the promise of good wages and decent housing and instead were often cheated out of pay and housed in dangerous slum-like labor camps. They were preyed upon by corrupt crew leaders and entrapped in a feudal system of manipulation and abuse that left them irrevocably mired in debt, while many of the growers outsourced any responsibility for them while reaping the benefits of their labor. Those who left the migrant stream remained in the area, mostly in Riverhead, and were forced to live, and in some cases die, in dangerous shacks or decrepit homes that sprang up in the absence of a proper housing code. This migratory labor system continued unabated for more than half a century and has undoubtedly left a stain on the legacy of Long Island.

Those in the system had competing interests, which made it impossible to reach a consensus on how to deal with the problem. The growers were beleaguered with their own troubles, which included an unstable agricultural market and suffocating environmental restrictions. Desperate for work that was scarce in the poverty-stricken South, most of the migrant workers continued to return each year, despite the abuse, squalor and danger that awaited them. The public was generally unaware of the complexity of the problems that occurred at labor camps discreetly placed miles away from town centers. Federal and state legislators refused to provide these workers with the protections of laws that left them vulnerable to abuse. Some local politicians remained callous or apathetic to the problem, while others held hearings and made lofty speeches demanding change. Regardless of their position, without any substantial public outcry over the problem, government officials were simply never compelled to make any true legislative changes.

Staunch individuals, social justice groups and diligent news reporters were well aware of the problem and urged the complete abolition of the system. However, with the county's high agricultural output and consistent lack of local manpower to fill the demands of the industry, total abolition was never truly a viable option. At a minimum, advocates called for the inclusion of farmworkers under the protection of federal or state labor laws. This was a viable plan that would have enabled migrant farmworkers to join labor unions that could have negotiated contracts on their behalf, providing fair wages and far better working conditions. Unfortunately, federal and state lawmakers never answered this desperate call. The fairly successful Puerto Rican contract model, which guaranteed prevailing wages and better working conditions, could have been adopted for all of the migrant laborers in the county. However, this model was used sparingly over the years before being completely abandoned by the cost-conscious growers.

Apportioning responsibility for this flawed system is challenging. There can be no doubt that the crew leaders served as both facilitators to and scapegoats of this migratory labor system. Without enough local help, the growers relied on crew leaders to procure a pool of workers each harvest season. In doing so, the growers willingly ceded all responsibility to the crew leaders, who exerted full control over labor, housing and most other aspects of the workers' lives. Moreover, worsening camp conditions were of little consequence to crew leaders, who only served in their roles seasonally before returning to their homes in other states.

Ultimately, the crew leaders do deserve a great deal of the blame, and their ruthless corruption is condemnable. However, there was and is enough fault to go around. By outsourcing all responsibility to the crew leaders while reaping the benefits of the labor pool despite worsening conditions, the growers also deserve their share in the blame. While deep-rooted families like the Wickham's generally treated their farmworkers with dignity and provided adequate housing for them, they were in the minority in comparison to the profit-driven growers who established the labor camps with little regard for the suffering of their inhabitants. Lastly, unlike California, there were no marches, strikes or widespread public outcry on Long Island demanding a change in the conditions of migrant workers. Instead, the public remained largely ignorant or indifferent to the problem. As a result, state and county officials were never compelled, and ultimately refused, to take any remedial action. Thus while the crew leader is an appropriate villain in this story, that role simply could not have existed without the willing participation, outright failure or sheer indifference of the growers, the surrounding communities and the local governments, who all share in the blame for this migratory labor system.

In 1960, the late Edward R. Murrow urged wage, health and housing reforms for migrant workers nationwide. Eight years later, the documentary *What Harvest for the Reaper?* confirmed that the migrant condition "is still the shame of the nation." In retrospect, the migratory labor system in Suffolk

County is representative of an industry that became more important than human life, where profit was paramount and exploitation all too common. That this system would thrive for as long as it did in one of the most affluent counties in the country undoubtedly leaves a shameful and lasting legacy.

It took more than half a century for the peak period of migrant labor camps on Long Island to vanish. Sadly, this demise was not fueled by a collective call to remedy the plight of the migrant workers. Instead, it was a combination of increased mechanization, a shifting farming ideology and a sharp increase in real estate prices, which ultimately led to a decline in potato production and the need for manpower, thus leading to the demise of the labor camps. As such, Lee Dennison might have been correct when he stated that the migrant worker situation corrected itself. Unfortunately, that provided little comfort to those who languished in this broken system for so many years.

On June 19, 2019, New York State passed the Farm Laborers Fair Labor Practices Act.[370] This law went into effect on January 1, 2020, and allows farmworkers to join labor unions and sets standards for working conditions for all farmworkers in the state.[371] The law is currently being subjected to legal challenges by the agricultural industry and has a long way to go before fulfilling its true purpose, but it is promising. Sadly, for people like Dilsia Trent and her three children, Myrtle Lee Grant, Spanish Magee and the others who perished, along with the thousands of migrant workers who languished in Long Island's migrant labor camps, this law arrived far too late.

BETTER ANGELS

The migratory labor system of the twentieth century was a dark period in the history of Suffolk County. However, during that time, there were advocates, both in their individual capacities and through their respective organizations, who refused to stand idly by and allow the mistreatment of migrant farmworkers to go unchallenged. As they strived to combat and improve the conditions of the labor camps, they were at times met with public ridicule, professional retribution and, in some cases, even threats of physical harm. Nevertheless, they persisted and have embodied the better angels of our nature. This section pays homage to some of those individuals.

ARTHUR CULLEN BRYANT

Arthur Cullen Bryant was born on April 3, 1928, in Brooklyn, New York.[372] Later, he attended Stuyvesant High School in Manhattan. Bryant spent his summers as a commercial fisherman alongside his stepfather, shipping out of various ports in the Northeast for weeks at a time to earn money for college. In 1949, he graduated from Gettysburg College and then answered the call to go into the ministry. As a young seminarian, he met Marion Maloney, who was born and raised in Queens, New York, and the couple married in 1951.

Bryant graduated from the Philadelphia Lutheran Theological Seminary with a master of divinity in 1953, and a short time later, he settled with his

St. Peter's Lutheran Church at its original location on Fifth Avenue in Greenport, New York. Toward the end of the 1960s, the church was relocated approximately three miles away to Main Road, where it continues to serve parishioners today. Reverend Arthur C. Bryant was the pastor in this church from 1960 to 1971. *Courtesy of David Corwin, Carlos DeJesus, and Gail Horton.*

family in the small town of Central Bridge, New York, where he served at Bethany Lutheran Church. In 1958, the Bryants relocated to the eastern end of Long Island after he answered the call to serve as pastor in St. Peter's Lutheran Church in the village of Greenport and Advent Lutheran Church in nearby Mattituck.

Reverend Bryant led a life of compassion and advocacy for impoverished people and especially farmworkers. His daughter Pamela stated, "My dad lived and died for helping the migrant workers." Bryant deeply appreciated the commonalities between his experiences as a commercial fisherman and a migrant farmworker. "We [fishermen] knew what it meant to work under a crew leader who can break watches at will and cause us to work 3 or 4 days without sleep," he stated. "We knew what it meant to be far away from home with no way of escape under harsh conditions."[373]

Reverend Bryant's appearance in June 1969 before a Senate committee proved to be the driving force in bringing nationwide attention to the plight of farmworkers in Suffolk County, which at the time was largely an isolated and local problem. He continued to speak on numerous television and radio programs, including televised appearances with fellow guest Dolores

Huerta, a founder of the United Farm Workers, and on a conservative talk show with host Alan Burke alongside guests Muhammad Ali and musician Frank Zappa. Bryant's efforts drew scorn and even threats to him and his family. During late night telephone calls, he was called a "nigger loving pastor."[374] Despite the vitriol he faced, Bryant relentlessly pursued the improvement or outright abolishment of the migratory labor system in Suffolk County.

In 1971, Reverend Arthur Bryant announced that he was departing Greenport after accepting a call to serve as pastor at the Augustana Lutheran Church in the Hyde Park neighborhood of Chicago, Illinois. On January 24, 1971, parishioners filled the pews of St. Peter's Lutheran Church to hear him deliver his final sermon.[375] "It's been a beautiful 15 years in Greenport," he said in front of the church's pulpit, shaped like the bow of a boat, which he helped to design. He then quoted from the book of Ecclesiastes, stating, "Whatever your hand finds it to do, do with all your might." Of his departure, one local reporter stated, "He was a very controversial figure. But there's a need for a man, who when he sees injustice done, doesn't bite his tongue or stick it in his cheek, but speaks out."[376]

In Illinois, Bryant worked in many capacities and continued to advocate for exploited farmworkers. After serving his parish in Chicago from 1971 to 1974, he served in the St. James Lutheran Church in Vandalia, Illinois, as well as the Zion Lutheran Church in Loogootee, Illinois. He was also the president of the Fayette County Genealogical Society and the Vandalia Ministerial Society. One day, Bryant was invited to join his daughter's fifth grade class to discuss his work and present the documentary *What Harvest for the Reaper?* to the young students. During the presentation, one of the students was particularly interested and had many questions. That student was none other than Maria Hinojosa, who would go on to become an award-winning journalist, producer and author. "It changed me," said Hinojosa, who reflected on the experience that helped shape her interest in human rights issues at such a young age. In her twenty-five years of work, Hinojosa has tirelessly produced community-based journalism to tell stories that are often underreported.[377] To inspire someone so young who went on to have an extraordinary career of advocacy is a fine example of Arthur Bryant's enduring legacy.

Arthur Bryant was a devoted husband who became a caregiver for his wife who was stricken with cancer and a loving father. On June 11, 1979, Bryant was outside his home mowing the yard when he suffered a sudden heart attack. He was rushed to Fayette County Hospital, where he later died.

Reverend Arthur Cullen Bryant in Vandalia, Illinois, in the early 1970s with a small bird perched on his right forearm. Bryant's daughter Pamela stated that her father "lived and died fighting for migrant workers." *Courtesy of the Bryant family.*

He was fifty-one years old. He was survived by his wife, Marion; children, Arthur, Eileen, Grace, Pamela and Maureen; and two grandchildren.

Reverend Arthur Bryant was a man of God, a teacher and a loving husband and father. He will also be remembered as a fearless warrior and outspoken critic of the migratory labor system in Suffolk County and throughout the country. His efforts greatly inspired me to research and tell this untold story.

HELEN WRIGHT PRINCE

There were few people who strived more for the well-being and nurturing of the children of migrant farmworkers in Suffolk County than Helen Wright Prince. From 1949 to 1961, Prince was a teacher at a makeshift school at the Cutchogue labor camp, the only known labor camp school in the state of New York.

Prince's role as a teacher is well documented in records held at the Southold Historical Society. However, her efforts as a caregiver to migrant children entrusted in her care was equally special. In the following passage from her 1989 memoir, *My Migrant Labor Camp School 1949–1961*, Prince recalls the times when she and her husband would bring the children to the beach of the nearby Long Island Sound:

> *Several times on lovely fall days I had the children get permission from their parents beforehand, and my husband would pile the children in the back of the pick-up, and we'd take them to the Sound beach at noon.... They simply delighted in tucking up their skirts and rolling up their pants and wading in the water. They would squeal and scream and talk about it. Some got a little too wet by accident, but they always stayed within the bounds set. They climbed on the very large rocks, skipped and threw stones, or climbed the steep sand cliff and ran screaming down. They darted from one delight to another as it was discovered. There was always something new for them on the beach: the shell of a horseshoe crab, unusual seaweed, a beautiful stone, orange and yellow jingle shells, conch shells worn to spirals, or driftwood gray and satiny. They would run up to me with these treasures and deposit them around me in growing piles. Sometimes we could do something with them, like making a jingle shell necklace or a stone exhibit, but more often we just left them there, happy to have had them for this fleeting moment.* [378]

Helen Prince was also a teacher at Southold Elementary School and devoted a great deal of time at the Suffolk County and Southold Historical Societies, where she preserved important history and kept meticulous records detailing her work. [379]

On May 1, 2013, Helen Wright Prince died peacefully. She was 101 years old. She was survived by her two sons, Bill and Barry Prince. In 2015, an event was sponsored by the Anti-Bias Task Force to celebrate her tireless work on behalf of the town of Southold. At the event, Southold town supervisor Scott Russell stated, "Sometimes we tend to overlook the small stuff to get to the bigger stuff and that's a shame, because in my experience in American history, I've found you need to look at those, because that's where the heroes were. People like Helen Prince. They were the heroes." To many people in Southold, and particularly the migrant children at the Cutchogue labor camp, Mrs. Prince was a hero indeed.

MARY CHASE STONE

Mary Chase came from a well-established New England family whose roots can be traced to the early settlers. Her father and mother both came from well-educated and service-oriented families and passed on these traditions to their children.

Mary Chase was not content with living a comfortable life. As a young adult, she became active in social justice programs. By the end of high school, she served in the Frontier Nursing Service, where she traveled by horseback to the poverty-stricken mountainous regions of Kentucky to assist families with childbirth and food preparation. After college, she trained as a progressive childhood education teacher and taught at several elementary schools in the New York area.

Early in World War II, Mary Chase married, had two children and settled on Long Island, where she continued to be very active in civic-service programs, including campaigning for President Dwight D. Eisenhower in 1952 and 1956. Later divorced, Mary raised her two children in a converted loft barn and lived a frugal life. Her daughter explained that her mother would purchase only essential items.

In describing the charitable nature of Mary Chase Stone, Laurence Hewes, a former attorney and friend of the family, stated, "She was sensitized to gross inequities in our society and wanted to take action." In 1960, Mary embarked on a mission with her two children and several other teenagers to help underprivileged migrant workers in Riverhead.[380] Each day, they traveled more than two hours to and from Riverhead in a station wagon with a five-gallon gasoline can strapped to the roof. Within two years, Mary went on to form the nonprofit organizations Long Island Volunteers and Seasonal Employees in Agriculture, both of which focused on providing food and searched for lodging for many of the migrant workers in the area. The group also provided self-improvement courses that taught various trades, such as auto mechanics, construction, adult literacy and family life.[381] In addition, Mary provided scheduling and transportation for medical and prenatal care. Mary also helped teach the children of the migrant workers how to read and served as a caregiver when, during the summer months, Mary's daughter and the other young volunteers took the children to the beach for varied recreation. "We loved them," her daughter fondly recalled.

Under Mary's leadership, Long Island Volunteers developed professional relationships with various federal, state and local agencies. Some of these

Mary Chase Stone in 1972. Mrs. Stone was the founder of Long Island Volunteers, the first nonprofit group to secure federal funding for a migrant program on Long Island. *Personal collection.*

groups included the Farmers Home Administration of the U.S. Department of Agriculture, the Job Corps and the Suffolk County Health Department, which were occasionally allowed to use the Long Island Volunteers headquarters.

For several years, Long Island Volunteers and other advocacy groups in the area debated over how to get federal funding for migrant workers. Squabbles between the groups appeared to have slowed the process, which frustrated Mary, who realized the importance of the funds. "She was not intolerant," Hewes stated. "She treated people as equals even though she had a commanding presence, but once she was clear in her goals, she could not be stopped."

Finally, in November 1965, Long Island Volunteers applied for a federal grant under the migrant program provision under the Economic Opportunity Act. Although it requested a total of $325,403, in May 1966, the group was awarded $203,663 in aid, making it the first Long Island–based group to receive federal funding for a migrant program.[382]

Mary also attacked the crew leader system and routinely lambasted crew leaders who were abusing and manipulating migrant workers. She openly advocated for increased investigations at the migrant camps.[383] When necessary, she initiated legal action against several camp operators, who she believed were unfairly manipulating the migrant workers. Reverend Jack H. Alford, executive director of the Long Island Council of Churches, called Mary Chase Stone a "saint" and stated, "She was trying so hard to get justice for these men. She kept it up 24 hours a day, seven days a week trying to trace a family, trying to see what happens to a paycheck….It was almost a hopeless task, but she did win about seven court cases."[384]

Mary regularly spoke at venues and events, raising awareness on behalf of migrant workers. One evening, she was asked to summarize the motivations for her efforts. Reading from a speech she had prepared for a memorial service for Dr. Martin Luther King Jr., Mary stated, "I want to do my best, put on another shingle, put on another coat of paint, mend up the leak, shore up that corner. It won't last unless we care for it. Just as we look after our houses, we must look after America."[385]

Over time, funding for Long Island Volunteers began to dwindle, and Mary was the last remaining member of the group.[386] She continued her work on behalf of the migrant workers, until she was overcome with leukemia and died in November 1977. She was survived by her son and daughter. Laurence Hewes described Mary as "careful, kind, someone who stood up for the rights of others and was always willing to accept the consequences of her action. She had all the best qualities of a New Englander."

Sadly, and despite her heroic efforts on behalf of the poor, the death of Mary Chase Stone drew little public attention. At her eulogy, Reverend Alford stated, "She gave away all she had, even her life. Mrs. Stone lived as Jesus Christ has asked of us."[387] Mary Chase Stone will be remembered as a fierce advocate on behalf of the migrant workers on Long Island.

Josephine Watkins-Johnson

Josephine Watkins-Johnson was born in Richmond, Virginia, in 1921. By the age of two, her family relocated to Greenport, New York. As a young teenager, she began working as a domestic servant. She later worked long hours at the Barstow shipyard in Greenport while proudly raising her family. Years later, she went to school for cosmetology, became a licensed hairdresser and served as a director at the Swedish Institute of Massage in New York City. In the 1960s, Watkins-Johnson ran a thriving catering business and went on to become the first Black member of the Greenport school district and fought to implement a free lunch program. She explained that her motivation in life was to attain for her children the many things she was denied during her youth as a woman of color.

Watkins-Johnson had to overcome many difficulties, which forced her to live a life full of faith. She was told that she would not survive the birth of one of her children, but she did. In her late thirties, she was hospitalized for a rare blood disease, but she recovered. In 1988, she was diagnosed with stage four ovarian cancer, and in 2016, she suffered a stroke. In each instance, she survived. Watkins-Johnson and her family also endured racism and bigotry throughout much of her life. She recalled the activity of the local Ku Klux Klan, although she described that the group's attention was primarily focused "on the Catholics."

In 1963, Watkins-Johnson was moved to tears when Reverend Arthur Bryant asked her to join his congregation at St. Peter's First Lutheran

Josephine Watkins-Johnson was a lifelong resident of Greenport, New York, known for her generosity and warm hospitality. This photo was taken in her home in the early 1980s. *Courtesy of Donna Johnson.*

Church in Greenport. Her family became the first Black family to do so. Some of the parishioners frowned on this and even left the church for good, but Bryant believed in inclusion, and the Johnson family was grateful. Over the years, the two families shared a strong bond that continues today with their children.

Watkins-Joseph was very sensitive to the plight faced by migrant workers and did all that she could to help them. In the 1960s, she served as a teacher at one labor camp, a role she stated had angered some local farmers. Although the family lived in a modest home on Kaplan Avenue in Greenport, she always welcomed children of migrant laborers into her home for dinner and hospitality.

Year later, Josephine Watkins-Johnson became the first Black woman to be admitted into Peconic Landing, one of the most renowned assisted-living facilities in the nation, where she was beloved by all who cared for her. In 2008, she was featured as part of a Black History Month celebration for her years of service in the community.

On March 12, 2020, Josephine Watkins-Johnson died peacefully in her sleep. She was ninety-nine years and nine days old. Her body was laid to rest in Calverton, New York. Her daughter, Donna, stated, "She was a laborer in the Lord's vineyard for 99 years and she clothed the naked, she fed the hungry. She comforted those who experienced a loss of some type. She championed the underdog."[388] I was blessed with the opportunity to meet Josephine Watkins-Johnson a few months before her death. She was bright, compassionate and possessed a heartwarming smile. The impression she left on me and everyone she met, along with her efforts on behalf of migrant farmworkers, will forever be admired.

Alan Perl

Alan Perl was born in 1909 and raised in Brooklyn, New York. He graduated from Columbia Law School in 1931 and a short time later began his career as a staff attorney with the National Labor Relations Board in Washington, D.C. In that role, he successfully tried a long series of cases against national corporations like Ford Motor Company and General Electric, which secured the rights of workers of those companies. Over time, Perl became the regional director of the New York regional office of the National Labor Relations Board and held that position for seven years. In 1947, Perl resigned from his position with the National Labor Relations Board in protest over the passage of the Taft-Hartley Act, which he felt stripped many of the rights of unionized workers.

Perl then cofounded the law firm Strum & Perl, specializing in labor law and representing unionized workers.[389] One year later, Rexford Tugwell, the appointed governor of Puerto Rico, asked Perl to assist the Puerto Rican government in drafting labor laws to help boost the Puerto Rican economy. For more than thirty years, Perl served as an adviser to various governors of Puerto Rico. In this role, he used his skill of negotiation and contract drafting, driven by a genuine concern for working people, to secure labor contracts for thousands of Puerto Rican farmworkers to work throughout the mainland United States. These contracts guaranteed wages, work hours, health coverage and other benefits, none of which were ever available to the other workers in the migrant stream.

During a 1985 interview, Perl spoke of a fraudulent contractor who in February 1947 left Puerto Rican farmworkers stranded during a blizzard in Chicago without any work or proper clothing.[390] The Puerto Rican government paid to have these workers immediately returned and subsequently passed a law making it a crime to engage in labor contracts unless they were approved by the Puerto Rican secretary of labor. Occurrences like this drove the Puerto Rican government to hire Perl, whose expertise and character they trusted to ensure the care and proper placement of workers coming from the island.

Alan Perl, who served as the regional director of the National Labor Relations Board in New York from 1940 to 1947. He was later retained by the Puerto Rico Department of Labor to negotiate and draft labor contracts with farm associations to employ Puerto Rican farmworkers in Connecticut, New York and New Jersey. *Courtesy of Daniel Perl.*

In 1976, Alan Perl retired and moved to Sarasota, Florida, to enjoy the warmer climate. He fished and played golf until his death in 2002 at the age of ninety-three. He was survived by two children, Dr. Daniel Perl and Emily Perl Kingsley; three grandchildren; and one great-grandchild. Alan Perl will be remembered as a champion of workers' rights whose efforts doubtlessly served to protect against the abuse and manipulation of many workers in this country and, in particular, Puerto Rican farmworkers in Suffolk County during the twentieth century.

MORTON SILVERSTEIN

Edward R. Murrow's 1960 production *Harvest of Shame* shamed the nation over the mistreatment of farmworkers in this country. However, the migrant labor system in Suffolk County remained a relatively unknown and localized problem. That all changed with the 1968 release of *What Harvest for the Reaper?*, the riveting documentary produced by Morton Silverstein that exposed the conditions at the Cutchogue labor camp.

Born on December 6, 1929, in Brooklyn, New York, Morton Silverstein was an Emmy Award–winning documentarian who used film to promote a wide range of social justice issues.[391] He set his sights on a career in journalism early in life and attended the University of Miami. He enlisted in the army in 1953, and when a ranking officer asked who among his troop could use a typewriter, Silverstein gladly raised his hand. He later met Rita Katz, and the couple married in 1962 and resided in New York City.

Silverstein's work was praised by many notable journalists, including Jack Gould of the *New York Times*, who called his documentary a "superb sequel" to *Harvest of Shame*. In 1970, Silverstein produced *Banks and the Poor*, an exposé on the relationship between the U.S. Congress and the banking industry. Over the years, Silverstein also produced socially conscious films such as *Eye On: Industrial Cancer, America at Risk: A History of Consumer Protest, The Poor Pay More* and *Death on the Highway*. He once described the inspiration for his work as being driven by a "sense of outrage at people being exploited and people without voices."

Morton Silverstein died on October 9, 2016. He was eighty-six years old. He was survived by his wife, Rita; daughter, Erika; and two grandchildren. Of his work, Silverstein once said, "If it ever turns out that everything is hunky-dory, that there was simply nothing to investigate, we'd call off the infantry. But I can't think of an instance where that's occurred." He further added, "I don't necessarily believe that there were always two sides to a story. There is only one side to the truth."

What Harvest for the Reaper? is one of the few tangible pieces of remaining evidence that depicts, with vivid clarity, the conditions at one of the largest labor camps in New York State. For this and his other work, Morton Silverstein will be remembered and praised for his contributions to this critical history.

HARVEY ARONSON

Harvey Aronson was born on May 17, 1929, and raised in Queens, New York. For most of his life, he wanted to be a writer. As a young child, he wrote poetry and short stories. In high school, he won a borough-wide essay contest about the United Nations and was honored with a prestigious award from Eleanor Roosevelt, an honor that remains one of the proudest moments of his life. Later, he attended Syracuse University for a degree in journalism; was a regular contributor to the school's newspaper, the *Daily Orange*; and later became the president of the Waiters' and Waitress' Union.

After earning his degree, Harvey was drafted by the U.S. Army and was sent to Germany during the Korean War. Two years later, he returned and married his college sweetheart, and the couple settled on Long Island. A short time later, Harvey began working at *Newsday*, where he became a feature writer and columnist. Harvey was one of the first journalists to chronicle the plight of migrant laborers on Long Island's East End in the 1950s. In August 1961, he authored a five-part series for *Newsday*, titled "Long Island's Migrants," which chronicled the conditions of the camps and proposed solutions to the problem.

Harvey went on to cover some of the biggest events of the time, from presidential campaigns and the civil rights movement to school integration in the South and discrimination against Black people in northern cities. Harvey has authored seven books, both fact and fiction, which include *High Hopes: The Amityville Murders* and *Naked Came the Stranger*. In a career that has spanned more than sixty years, Harvey Aronson was inducted into the Long Island Journalism Hall of Fame. In 2004, he joined the founding faculty of the School of Journalism at Stonybrook University. In 2018, Harvey retired, and as of this writing, at ninety-one years old, he is currently working on a new book about his father.

Harvey Aronson was a pioneer in the coverage of migrant labor camps on Long Island. His efforts helped to preserve a history that was nearly lost, and for his efforts and stellar career, he is rightfully honored in this book.

STEVE WICK

Steve Wick was born in Camden, New Jersey, in 1951. He eventually settled on Long Island and has spent nearly four decades as a reporter and editor. Wick began his career at *Newsday* in 1978, and he went on to win dozens of awards, including sharing in two Pulitzer Prize awards and the Outstanding Long Island Journalist Award in 2010 for local reporting. His work includes local history series and supervising a two-year project documenting the lives of caregivers for Alzheimer's patients. Steve is also the author of several books, including *Heaven and Earth: The Last Farmers of the North Fork*.

As of this writing, Steve works as the executive editor of the Times Review Media Group, which publishes the *Suffolk Times*, the *Riverhead News-Review* and the *Shelter Island Reporter*. In 2017, Steve and fellow editor Grant Parpan helped revive and solve the fifty-one-year-old unsolved murder of Louise Pietrewicz of Cutchogue, New York. Their report included a video documentary, *Gone: The Disappearance of Louise Pietrewicz*.

Journalist Steve Wick currently serves as the executive editor of the Times Review Media Group, which publishes the *Suffolk Times*, the *Riverhead News-Review* and the *Shelter Island Reporter*. He is an award-winning reporter who wrote extensively on migrant farmworkers on Long Island. *Courtesy of Steve Wick.*

Over the years, Steve has authored a number of riveting articles about the migrant labor camps in Cutchogue and throughout the North Fork. I will forever be appreciative to Steve for the time he spent with me as I researched this topic, including a visit to Cox Lane in Cutchogue, where we stood directly in front of the site of the notorious labor camp and discussed this dark history.

Steve was one of the few reporters who was present in the waning days of a labor camp on Depot Lane, not far from the location of the notorious labor camp in Cutchogue. It was the very last of its kind, in an area known to once have dozens of similar camps. Steve did much more than reporting. Over the years, be befriended a former migrant worker named Jimmy Wilson, who was in his eighties and worked at that camp and many others since he was a teenager. "In all these conversations," stated Wick, "he never showed any concern that one day the life he had known all these years would die out and he would be stranded."[392]

In 2006, when a fire destroyed one of the last remaining potato processing plants in the area, which stood next to the labor camp, Steve sprang into action. He took two men who had spent all of their lives at camps, Oliver Burke and Frank Singleton, back to where they were born in Georgia and South Carolina, respectively. Oliver was reunited with his mother, who gave him up for adoption soon after his birth; Frank was reunited with his family, including his ninety-year-old mother, who had not seen her son in decades.

Steve learned that Jimmy Wilson was born in the tiny town of Barwick, Georgia. After the fire, Steve offered to take him back to his birthplace, since the camp was no longer in operation. Wilson always refused, but in June 2006, he asked Steve, "If you go, please find where my mother is buried and put flowers on her grave for me." Steve agreed. Wilson died of a heart attack just a few months later, just a few miles from the Cutchogue camp where he spent a large part of his life.

After Wilson's death, Steve worked to learn more about him. Death records in Georgia showed Mr. Wilson's mother, Ada Wilson, died in Barwick in 1925, when her son was six years old. He learned that after the death of his mother, Wilson moved to northern Florida with his grandmother, Julia Wilson. When she died in 1932, Jimmy, barely in his teens and desperate for work, climbed aboard a truck bound for New Jersey, where he worked for years at a farm in Red Bank. In 1948, he moved to Port Jefferson, New York, where he worked in a potato grading barn. After a fire killed two of his friends, Wilson moved out to the North Fork, where he remained for the rest of this life.

Steve continued his search and eventually located Wilson's relatives in Georgia, where he told them about Wilson. On a Sunday morning, Steve Wick stood with Mr. Wilson's cousin Belle Williams, who placed a bouquet of flowers on Ada Wilson's grave, fulfilling the promise that he made to Wilson before he died. It was an extraordinary display of humanity from a journalist who has spent much of his life reporting the plight of migrant workers in Suffolk County and befriending some of them, including Oliver, Frank and Mr. Wilson.

(*Top, left*): I.M. Young potato field planted with "early potatoes," which are harvested in August, circa 1973. *Courtesy of the Eastern Farm Workers Association.* (*Top, right*): Eastern Farm Workers Association members at the I.M. Young Labor Camp in Cutchogue, New York. Date unknown. *Courtesy of the Eastern Farm Workers Association.* (*Middle*): I.M. Young's main potato grading shed on Osbourne Avenue and Route 58 in Riverhead, New York, circa 1973. *Courtesy of the Eastern Farm Workers Association.* (*Bottom*): The I.M. Young labor camp in Riverhead, New York. Note the "private keep out" sign, circa 1973. *Courtesy of the Eastern Farm Workers Association.*

LABOR CAMP INDEX

The following index contains the names of migrant labor camps that, according to the Suffolk County Department of Health and other public records, operated at some point between 1943 and 2000. Unless specifically referenced in this book, the author makes no representation about the conditions of any labor camp in this index at any time or against any of the owners, operators or inhabitants of any labor camp in this index or elsewhere.

Facility	Location	Town/Hamlet
Abramowski Farm	Mount Sinai Road	Mount Sinai
Agway Labor Camp	Edgar Avenue	Aquebogue
Agway Labor Camp	Osborne Avenue	Riverhead
Agway Labor Camp	Sound Avenue	Mattituck
Agway Labor Camp	Sound Avenue	Peconic
A.J. Schmitt Farms	Ruland Road	Melville
Albert Schmitt and Son	New Highway	Farmingdale
Albert Schmitt and Son	Old East Neck Road	Melville
Albert Schmitt Farms	Laurel Lane	Laurel
Amagansett Farm	Main Street	Amagansett

Facility	Location	Town/Hamlet
Anderson Labor Camp	South Harbor Road	Southold
Anthony Babinski Farm	Mecox Road	Bridgehampton
Baldwin Labor Camp	Foster Avenue	Bridgehampton
Barbato Brothers	Mount Pleasant Road	Smithtown
Beamon Labor Camp	Kroemer Avenue	Calverton
Beanery Labor Camp	Menantic Road	Shelter Island
Bergold and Wakefield	Mount Sinai Road	Mount Sinai
Bernstein Boulevard Nursery	Bernstein Boulevard	Center Moriches
Bissett Nursery	Henry Street	Farmingville
Bolling Labor Camp	Queen Street	Greenport
Brand Nurseries	Park Avenue	Huntington
Briarcliff Sod	Henry Street	Farmingville
Briermere Farm	Sound Avenue	Riverhead
Brigman Labor Camp	Queen Street	Greenport
Bruno Beck Labor Camp	unknown	Port Jefferson
Bulk's Nurseries	Montauk Highway	Babylon
Bushwick Labor Camp	Railroad Avenue	Jamesport
(A.C.) Carpenter Labor Camp	Deerfield Road	Water Mill
Casa De Lalio Farms	Cooper Street	Shoreham
Cassidy Farm Labor Camp	Cox Lane	Cutchogue
Coastal Greenhouses	Sound Avenue	Shoreham
Colonial Springs Nursery	Sixteenth Street	Babylon
Corwith Farms	Narrow Lane	Bridgehampton
Coty Labor Camp	unknown	Northhampton
Country Gardens	Locust Avenue	East Moriches
Country Gardens	Old Country Road	Eastport
Country Gardens	L.I. Expressway	Melville

Facility	Location	Town/Hamlet
Davis Farm	Deer Park Avenue	Huntington
Deer Run Farms	South Country Road	Brookhaven
Delea Labor Camp	Elwood Road	East Northport
Della Jackson Labor Camp	unknown	Calverton
Demarest Labor Camp	Main Road (Route 25)	Orient
Duroski Labor Camp	Ackerly Pond Lane	Southold
Eastern Potato Dealers Labor Camp	unknown	Aquebogue
Eastern Suffolk Coop.	Cox Lane	Cutchogue
Eberhard Nurseries	Pine Street	East Moriches
Edwin Gould Foundation Camp	unknown	Kings Park
E.L. Briggman Labor Camp	unknown	Greenport
Erb Labor Camp	Burrs Lane	Huntington
Fargo Labor Camp	Laurel Lane	Laurel
Farmers Exchange	Osborne Avenue	Riverhead
Finn and Sons Labor Camp	Wellwood Avenue	Pinelawn
Fisher's Island Utility Company	Crescent Avenue	Fisher's Island
Fox Hollow Farm	Sound Avenue	Calverton
Frank Salters Labor Camp	Sound Avenue and Cox Neck Road	Mattituck
George Szczepanowksi Labor Camp	unknown	Bridgehampton
Gordon Hospital (former site)	unknown	Port Jefferson
Greenport Labor Camp	Country Road 48	Greenport
H.F. McKay Labor Camp	Sound Avenue	Riverhead

Facility	Location	Town/Hamlet
Half Hollow Nursery North	Main Road (Route 25)	Laurel
Half Hollow Nursery South	Main Road (Route 25)	Laurel
Halsey Labor Camp	unknown	Northhampton
Hartman Labor Camp	Reeves Avenue	Riverhead
Henry Jacobs Labor Camp	Foster Avenue	Bridgehampton
Holly Hollow	unknown	Peconic
I.M. Young Labor Camp	Foster Avenue	Bridgehampton
I.M. Young Labor Camp	Edwards Avenue	Calverton
I.M. Young Labor Camp	Depot Lane	Cutchogue
I.M. Young Labor Camp	Osborne Avenue	Riverhead
I.M. Young Labor Camp	Youngs Avenue	Southold
Imperial Nurseries	Miller Place Road	Miller Place
Island Potato	Sound Avenue	Riverhead
Jackson Labor Camp	Manorville Road	Wading River
John Brigati Farms	unknown	Huntington
John Gozelski Cabor Camp	unknown	East Northport
Joseph Borella Labor Camp	Moriches Road	Brookhaven
Kalba Labor Camp	unknown	Wading River
Krupski Labor Camp	Bridge Lane	Cutchogue
Kurt Weiss	Oregon Road	Mattituck
Kurt Weiss	Montauk Highway	Brookhaven
Lake Grove Labor Camp	Stony Brook Road	Stony Brook
Lake Lodge Labor Camp	unknown	Peconic
Lappe Labor Camp	South Harbor Road	Southold
Latham Farms	Main Road (Route 25)	Orient

LABOR CAMP INDEX

Facility	Location	Town/Hamlet
Latham Farms West	Main Road (Route 25)	Orient
Laurel Hill Nurseries	Mount Sinai-Coram Road	Mount Sinai
Lee Labor Camp	Main Road (Route 25)	Mattituck
Lewin Farms	Sound Avenue	Calverton
Lewinard Sones	Sound Avenue	Wading River
Liere Brothers	Long Island Avenue	Yaphank
Lipco-Agway Labor Camp	Edgar Avenue	Aqeubogue
Lohman Labor Camp	South Country Road	Brookhaven
Long Island Cauliflower	Mill Road	Riverhead
Long Island Cauliflower	Osborne Avenue	Riverhead
Lustgarten Nurseries	Route 25	Middle Island
Marders Butterlane Nurseries	Butterlane Road	Bridgehampton
Marie Jackson Labor Camp	Manorville-Wading River Road	Wading River
McGovern Sod Farms	Pinelawn Road	Melville
McKasty Labor Camp	unknown	Yaphank
McKay Labor Camp	Osborne Avenue	Riverhead
Milton Warner Labor Camp	Parker Road	Wading River
Mish Farm Labor Camp	Edgewood Avenue	St. James
Muller Labor Camp	unknown	Huntington
Myron Nelson Labor Camp	Old Quogue Road	Riverhead
Ngen Lee Farm	unknown	Calverton
Noah Halsey Labor Camp	Vail Avenue	Riverside
Northeast Nurseries	Country Road 48	Cutchogue
North Fork Nursery	Herricks Lane	Jamesport
North Fork Nursery	Depot Lane	Cutchogue

Facility	Location	Town/Hamlet
North Shore Produce	Edgar Avenue	Aquebogue
Nowaski Labor Camp	unknown	Miller Place
Parmeintier's Labor Camp	Grady Street	Bayport
Peikowski Labor Camp	unknown	Huntington
Peters Labor Camp	unknown	Gordon Heights
Pinewood Nursery	Sterling Lane	Cutchogue
Pollack Labor Camp	Edgar Avenue	Bridgehampton
Pollack Labor Camp	Columbia Street	Port Jefferson Station
Pollack Labor Camp	unknown	Riverhead
Quality Plants	unknown	Brookhaven
Quality Plants	Brookfield Avenue	Center Moriches
Quality Plants	Northern Boulevard	Shirley
Quality Plants	Moriches-Yaphank Road	Manorville
Quality Plants	Maplewood Road	Shirley
Reeves Avenue Labor Camp	Reeves Avenue	Riverhead
Riverside Labor Camp	Old Quogue Road	Riverhead
Rosko Labor Camp	Butter Lane	Bridgehampton
Rosko Labor Camp	Powell Avenue	Southampton
Rothman's Pickle Works	unknown	East Northport
Rottkamp	Wellwood Avenue	Huntington
Sacks and Sons Labor Camp	Montauk Highway	Bridgehampton
Sacks and Sons Labor Camp	unknown	Mattituck
Sacks and Sons Labor Camp	Osborne Avenue	Riverhead
Sang Lee Farms	Head of Neck Road	East Moriches

Facility	Location	Town/Hamlet
Santorelli Brothers	East Northport Road	Kings Park
Sayre Baldwin Labor Camp	Butter Lane	Bridgehampton
Schrakamp-Kemper Nurseries	Larkfield Road	East Northport
Schrakamp-Kemper Nurseries	Mills Pond Road	St. James
Sepenoski Labor Camp	Main Road (Route 25)	East Marion
Setauket Farms	Route 25A	Setauket
Short Labor Camp	Old Quogue Road	Southampton
Silbertstein Farm	Elwood Road	East Northport
Sledjeski Labor Camp	Main Road (Route 25)	Orient
Sommer Nurseries	Old Country Road	Eastport
South Shore Produce	unknown	Bridgehampton
South Shore Produce	Narrows Lane	Wainscott
Southampton Produce	Montauk Highway	Bridgehampton
Stanco Labor Camp	Gardiner Avenue	East Hampton
Stanley Detmers Labor Camp	unknown	East Setauket
Still Farm Labor Camp	unknown	Coram
Tabor Labor Camp	Orchard Street	Orient
Tabor Labor Camp	Hallock Road	Orient
Terry Labor Camp	Main Road (Route 25)	Orient
Warner Nursery	Sound Avenue	Calverton
Wesnofske Labor Camp	Foster Avenue	Bridgehampton
Wesnofske Labor Camp	Cook's Lane	Bridgehampton
Wicks (George Jr.) Farm	Furman Road	Greenlawn
Wicks Nurseries	unknown	Huntington
Wicks Nurseries	Main Road (Route 25)	Jamesport
Wicks Nurseries	unknown	Laurel

LABOR CAMP INDEX

Facility	Location	Town/Hamlet
Wicks Nurseries	unknown	Miller Place
Wicks Nurseries	unknown	Wading River
Woodbourne Nurseries	unknown	Huntington
Woodbourne Nurseries	unknown	Melville
Woodlea Nursery	First Avenue	Moriches
Wright Labor Camp	Mill Road	Riverhead
Zahler Labor Camp	Edgar Avenue	Aquebogue

NOTES

Introduction

1. Cashman, "Migrants Die in LI ."
2. "Tragedy Spurs Aid to Migrant Labor," *Newsday*, November 26, 1950.
3. "Riverhead Slum Fire Kills Man; Town Acts," *Newsday*, February 4, 1959.
4. "3 Children Killed in Shanty Blaze," *Newsday*, January 30, 1959.
5. "Slum Fire Kills Riverhead Man; 7th Victim of '59," *Newsday*, June 15, 1959.
6. "2 Babies Die in Fire," *Suffolk County News*, May 2, 1963.
7. "Grand Jury Won't Investigate Blaze," *East Hampton Star*, February 1, 1968.
8. "A 20th Century Form of Slavery," *Newsday*, November 21, 1968.

Chapter 1

9. "Long Island," Britannica.
10. Hallocks Farm Museum, Riverhead, New York.
11. Fleming and Folk, "Munnawhatteaug."
12. "A Fruitful Harvest; 36 years of Tending Suffolk's Farms," *Newsday*, December 16, 1971.
13. Hallocksville Farm Museum, Riverhead, New York.
14. "Suffolk County to Have Farm Bureau," *East Hampton Star*, December 16, 1916.

15. "Potatoes Are Prime Long Island Crop," *Patchogue Advance*, January 20, 1949.
16. Wages and Wage Rates of Potato Harvest Workers on Long Island, September 1, 1945, U.S. Department of Agriculture, Bureau of Agricultural Economics.
17. "The Last Potato Graders," *Newsday*, April 2, 2005.
18. Bracero History Archive. The Bracero program was extended under President Truman with the signing of the Migratory Labor Agreement of 1951. After years of controversy and the mistreatment of millions of farmworkers, the program was terminated on December 1, 1964.
19. "Seek 3,400 Farm Workers for Long Island Harvest," *Newsday*, May 12, 1942.
20. "Text of Dewey's Address on Farm Manpower," *Newsday*, February 26, 1943.
21. "State to Recruit, Train 30,000 Farm Workers," *Newsday*, February 10, 1943.
22. "Suffolk Farmers May Lose Their Jamaican Help," *Suffolk County News*, August 13, 1943.
23. "Recruiting of Labor for Farms Discussed," *New York Times*, April 12, 1943.
24. "Suffolk Gets German Prisoners," *New York Times*, August 2, 1945.
25. "Eastern Suffolk Cooperative Decides to Employ Polish DP's for Farm Help," *Long Island Traveler*, April 21, 1949; "Suffolk Farmers to Hire Refugees," *New York Times*, April 17, 1949.
26. "L.I. Farm Bureau Backs Youth Harvest Workers," *Patchogue Advance*, March 24, 1960. According to federal law, no child under the age of sixteen could be employed on farms. In New York, children under fourteen years old were prohibited from farm work, but children between fourteen and sixteen years of age could perform farm labor only during the summer months when there was no school and after undergoing a physical examination from a doctor; "U.S. Watching Island Farmers for Child Labor," *Patchogue Advance*, May 24, 1951.
27. "Suffolk Airs Issue of Farm Migrants," *New York Times*, June 11, 1953.
28. "Plan to Import Jamaicans to Work on Farms," *County Review*, June 10, 1943.
29. "Suffolk Farmers May Lose Their Jamaican Help," *Suffolk County News*, August 13, 1943.
30. "All Jamaicans Leave Suffolk Farms; May Return to Help Again Next Year," *Suffolk County News*, November 12, 1943.
31. "600 Jamaicans to Work on County Farms," *Newsday*, May 22, 1945.
32. *Long Island Traveler*, September 11, 1947.

33. "First Puerto Rican Laborers Arrive for Work on L.I. Farms," *Advance*, July 15, 1948.
34. "First Puerto Rican Laborers Arrive for Work on L.I. Farms," *Patchogue Advance*, July 15, 1948; *East Hampton Star*, August 19, 1948.
35. Records that indicate that Suffolk County employed Mexican farmworkers under the Bracero Plan could not be located.
36. "Long Island's Migrants," *Newsday*, August 28, 1961.
37. "State Surveys Farm Housing for New Migrant Labor Code," *Newsday*, September 2, 1961.
38. "Harvest of Loneliness," *Newsday*, September 8, 1991.
39. "L.I. Migrants: Unresolved Plight," *Newsday*, June 23, 1972.

Chapter 2

40. National Labor Relations Board.
41. Ibid.
42. Reilly, "Agricultural Laborers."
43. *Hearings Before the Subcomm. on Migratory Labor of the Comm. on Labor and Public Welfare*, 90th Cong. 28, 44 (1969). (Hereafter cited as 1969 hearings.)
44. Oral interview by author with Burt Neuborne, August 21, 2020.
45. "Senator Proposes New Deal to Help Migrant Farm Hands," *Newsday*, March 1, 1961.
46. "Long Island's Migrants," *Newsday*, September 1, 1961.
47. "Migrant Rights Still Lag After 32 Years," *Newsday*, November 21, 1969.
48. New York State Department of Labor Report for 1943–48.
49. "Migrant Workers: A Challenge to Our Social Conscience," *Suffolk County News*, May 18, 1946.
50. "Dewey Signs into Law Labor Camp, RR Bills," *Advance*, April 8, 1954.
51. "Ave Tightens Health Rules at Migrant Labor Camps," *Newsday*, June 20, 1958. The regulations are detailed in the New York State Public Health Law, section 225, Part 15, titled "Migrant Farmworker Housing."
52. "New Sanitary Rules for Migrant Labor Camps," *Long Island Traveler*, December 18, 1958.
53. "LI Township Gets First Zoning Law," *New York Times*, April 14, 1957.
54. "Farm Labor Camp Sites Picked," *New York Times*, March 12, 1942.
55. "Riverhead Rejects Farm Labor Camp," *New York Times*, June 23, 1942.
56. "Okay Farm Camp, State Labor Only," *County Review*, March 11, 1943.
57. "Protest Farm Labor Camps," *County Review*, October 31, 1946.
58. "Oppose Farm Labor Camp," *County Review*, November 6, 1947.
59. *Long Island Traveler*, May 27, 1954.

60. *Suffolk County News*, May 18, 1956.

61. "Farm Labor Camp to Be Established in Southold for Jamaicans to Relieve Help Shortage on North Fork," *Long Island Traveler Mattituck Watchman*, June 10, 1943. Unlike the rejected proposal that was made in March 1943 to use American farmworkers from other states, this contract for foreign Jamaican workers from the British West Indies was sponsored by the U.S. government, who defrayed much of the costs. This would explain why approval for this camp was more easily granted.

62. "134 Migrant Labor Camps in Suffolk; Increase 5-fold," *Patchogue Advance*, May 21, 1959.

63. "A Vanishing Breed," *Sunday News*, May 25, 1969.

64. The Suffolk County Migrant Labor and Slum Housing Commission prepared a map in April 1960 that details how many labor camps existed in the ten towns of the county. They are as follows: Babylon (three), Brookhaven (twenty), East Hampton (two), Huntington (seventeen), Islip (one), Riverhead (thirty), Shelter Island (two), Smithtown (eight), Southampton (thirteen) and Southold (twenty-four).

65. Garcia-Colon, *Colonial Migrants*, 136. In 1943, there were a total of 287 labor camps in New York State. That number increased to 451 in 1948.

66. "L.I.'s Other People," *Newsday*, September 4, 1965; *Long Island Traveler*, April 24, 1969.

67. "Work Camp Abuses Cited," *Newsday*, October 28, 1975.

68. "More Fire Over Health Nominee," *Newsday*, May 24, 1985.

69. "Farm Labor Camp to Be Established in Southold for Jamaicans to Relieve Help Shortage on North Fork," *Long Island Traveler*, June 10, 1943.

70. "Poverty Covers Migrant Alley," *Newsday*, August 29, 1957.

71. "Long Island's Pockets of Poverty," *Newsday*, March 28, 1964.

Chapter 3

72. Squire, "Dark Days"; "Work near Completion on American Migrant Camp at Cutchogue," *Long Island Traveler*, July 11, 1946.

73. New York Department of State Division of Corporations.

74. "Cutchogue Sale," *County Review*, July 25, 1946.

75. "Work Near Completion on American Migrant Camp in Cutchogue," *Long Island Traveler*, July 11, 1946.

76. "New Men's Dormitory Opened at Cutchogue Labor Camp," *Long Island Traveler-Mattituck Watchman*, August 8, 1968.

77. Prince, "My Migrant Labor Camp School"; "Cutchogue Labor Camp Now Enlarged to House 175 Harvest Workers," *Long Island Traveler*, April 24, 1947.

78. Prince, "My Migrant Labor Camp."
79. Ibid.
80. "Probe LI 'Model' Migrant Camp," *Newsday*, August 31, 1957.
81. Wick, *Heaven and Earth*, 91.
82. "4 Migrants Die in a Fire at Cutchogue Labor Camp," *Long Island Traveler Mattituck Watchman*, October 12, 1961.
83. "LI's Other Summer People," *Newsday*, September 4, 1965.
84. "Migrant Worker Conditions," *Tucson Daily Citizen*, October 11, 1967.
85. *What Harvest for the Reaper?*
86. "Suffolk Urged to End Brutal Farm Labor System," *Newsday*, October 17, 1967.
87. *Long Island Traveler*, March 17, 1966.
88. "Quash Plan to House Migrants," *Newsday*, March 21, 1966.
89. "Farm Co-op to Evict State Day-Care Center," *Newsday*, September 10, 1966.
90. "Cutchogue Labor Camp Refused New Permit," *Long Island Traveler*, January 22, 1970.
91. "Dark Days at the Cutchogue Labor Camp," *Suffolk Times*, September 26, 2014.
92. Richard B. Conklin was a Greenport resident, merchant and horse breeder. The mansion was located on the North Road just east of Chapel Lane; "Preserving Local History," *Peconic Bay Shopper*, July 1, 2012.
93. *Long Island Traveler*, April 14, 1966.
94. "Labor Camp Proposed in Southold Town for Men to Work on Farms," *Long Island Traveler-Mattituck Watchman*, February 11, 1943.
95. *North Fork Life*, February 18, 1943.
96. Much of this information is derived from a public letter Edwin H. King wrote in the early 1960s to Southold residents as he campaigned, albeit unsuccessfully, for the office of councilman in the area. Mr. King died in 1970.
97. *Long Island Traveler*, October 19, 1950.
98. "Rains Boon to Suffolk Potato Crop," June 28, 1945.
99. *County Review*, May 27, 1948.
100. *Peconic Bay Shopper*, July 2012.
101. *Southampton Press*, July 11, 1947.
102. *Long Island Traveler*, September 11, 1947.
103. *Long Island Traveler*, July 31, 1958.
104. The site of the former camp is currently occupied by a nursing and rehabilitation center in Greenport.
105. For a complete list of the labor camps found during my research, please see the index in the back of this book. This index contains the names of

labor camps that were reported by the Suffolk County Department of Health and other public records to have operated between 1943 and 2000.

106. *North Fork Life,* July 1, 1943.

107. *Long Island Traveler-Mattituck Watchman,* January 17, 1957.

108. In 1949, the schoolhouse was relocated and today is occupied by the Oysterponds Historical Society.

109. Oral interview by author with Jerie Newman, granddaughter of Edwin H. King, July 25, 2020.

110. *Long Island Traveler-Mattituck Watchman,* November 21, 1957, and July 13, 1961.

111. Oral interview by author with Dan Latham, Southold Historical Society.

112. Oral interview by author with Doug Morris, lifelong resident of Greenport, July 25, 2020.

113. "Home at Last," *Newsday,* December 24, 2005.

114. "The Last Potato Graders: The End of the Line," *Newsday,* April 24, 2005.

115. "This Is the Last of It: Cutchogue Barn Fire Destroys Operation of Last Commercial Potato Grading Business on the Island," *Newsday,* May 2, 2006.

116. Before the fire, the barn was reportedly used by David Steele and Bobby Rutkoski of Mattituck and John Sepenoski of East Marion. The other remaining potato growers in the region bagged their own potatoes.

117. Oral interview by author with Tom Wickham, July 30, 2020.

118. Oral interview by author with Steve Wick, July 26, 2020.

119. "Migrants Find Little Cheer," *Newsday,* December 26, 1969.

120. "Getting to the Heart of Migrants' Woes," *Newsday,* December 3, 1970.

121. "LI Migrant Workers Living in Squalor," *Long Island Press,* April 28, 1969.

122. *Long Island Traveler-Mattituck Watchman,* December 11, 1975.

123. Under New York law, if a corporation does not voluntarily dissolve and fails to file franchise tax returns or pay franchise taxes for two or more years, the corporation is subject to dissolution by proclamation.

124. Sylvester Manor Educational Farm.

125. The Beanery Plant was located on what is today a vacant lot on South Ferry Road adjacent to the current location of the Shelter Island Historical Society.

126. "Island Industry Venture: The Old Beanery," *Shelter Island Reporter,* December 18, 1980.

127. Cooperative Aids Shelter Island, *Shelter Island Reporter,* 1950.

128. Jaicks, "Race, Ethnicity and Class."

129. "25 Homeless in Labor Camp Fire," *Southampton Press*, December 19, 1957.
130. *East Hampton Star*, February 13, 1968.
131. "E. Northport Raid Finds 30 Migrants in 1 House," *Newsday*, June 21, 1961.

Chapter 4

132. Lariccia and Tucciarone, "Bound for America."
133. "The Land Where Crew Chief Is Boss," *Newsday*, May 21, 1978.
134. "U.S. Government Licenses Violent Farm Crew Bosses," *Newsday*, October 3, 1983.
135. "U.S., State Probing LI Migrant Labor Abuses," *Newsday*, May 22, 1961.
136. "The Land Where Crew Chief Is Boss," *Newsday*, May 21, 1978.
137. *What Harvest for the Reaper?*
138. "Talking with Otis Johnson," *Newsday*, June 29, 1975.
139. "Land Where Crew Chief."
140. "Suffolk Urged to End Brutal Farm Labor System," *Newsday*, October 17, 1967.
141. "Land Where Crew Chief."
142. "A Boss Admits He Cheated Migrants," *Newsday*, June 27, 1972.
143. "Mary Chase Stone, 66, Friend of Riverhead Migrant Workers," *Newsday*, November 23, 1977.
144. "Boss Charged in Beatings of Migrants," *Newsday*, October 31, 1972.
145. "The Exploitation of Alfonzo Mahone, 15," *Newsday*, September 14, 1968.
146. "Puerto Rico Film Warns Migrants," *New York Times*, March 7, 1953.
147. Garcia-Colon, "Claiming Equality."
148. Aronson, "Long Island's Migrants."
149. "LI Migrants: Unresolved Plight," *Newsday*, June 23, 1972.
150. September 1960 Migrant Newsletter.

Chapter 5

151. Sherman and Levy, "Free Access to Migrant Labor," 434–37.
152. "Migrant Labor in the East," *New York Times*, August 29, 1960.
153. "Migrants," *Suffolk County News*, June 8, 1956.
154. 1969 hearings.
155. 1969 hearings, 29, 45.

156. 1969 hearings, 14, 30.
157. *Long Island Traveler*, July 24, 1952.
158. "L.I. Farmers Praise Migrant Hands' Crew Chief," *New York Times*, June 6, 1966.
159. Payne, "Waiting for the Eagle."
160. Tomkins and Tomkins, *Other Hampton*.
161. "Nuns Assist Year-Round Migrants," *New York Times*, February 25, 1973.
162. Rivera, "Migrants Dirt Cheap."
163. "High Illness Rate Found in Children of Migrants," *New York Times*, August 18, 1982.
164. "An Unmeasured Harvest of Poison," *Newsday*, October 10, 1973.
165. 1969 hearings, 12, 28.
166. *Harvest of Shame*.
167. "For Migrant Workers, It's a Cycle of Grading and Waiting," *New York Times*, December 20, 1981.
168. "Body of a Migrant Found at Mattituck," *Long Island Traveler Mattituck Watchman*, April 12, 1956.
169. "Farmhand Murdered in Mattituck on 22nd," *Long Island Traveler Mattituck Watchman*, December 30, 1965.
170. "State Units Probe LI Migrants' Death," *Newsday*, April 11, 1969.
171. "LI Migrant Worker Called a Hero at Memorial," *New York Times*, May 14, 1972.
172. Holley, "Disadvantaged by Design."
173. *Hearings Before the Subcomm. on Migratory Labor of the Comm. on Labor and Public Welfare*, 91st Cong., Pt. 8-A, 4, 984 (1970).)
174. "Farmers Harvest a Crop of Injuries Agriculture Tops Mining Risks," *Newsday*, October 30, 1990.
175. Ibid.
176. Employers with a yearly migrant payroll of greater than $1,200 were required to comply with the Workman's Compensation Act.
177. "Migrants Get Help, But Not Enough," *Newsday*, September 27, 1966.
178. "X-Rays for LI Migrants," *New York Times*, November 6, 1957.
179. "Government Grant to Aid County Migrant Health Project," *Long Island Traveler*, July 30, 1970.
180. "Suffolk Starts TB Testing for Migrants," *Newsday*, June 26, 1962; "Suffolk OK's Program for Migrant Aid," *Newsday*, May 25, 1965.
181. In 1963, the program was awarded a federal grant in the amount of $53,995, and in 1968 an additional grant of $46,340 was also awarded to the program; "Government Grant to Aid County Migrant Health Project," *Long Island Traveler*, July 30, 1970; "46,000 U.S. Grant for Migrants Here," *Long-Islander*, August 7, 1969.

182. Arthur Bryant, "Why Do I Go Around in Circles?"
183. "$5 Altercation Ends in Stabbing," *County Review*, September 16, 1948.
184. "Dorsey Told to Leave Here," *County Review*, November 18, 1948.
185. "Sacks Clear So Far on 'Bought' Beating," *Advance Patchogue*, August 4, 1955.
186. "Migrant Swears Spud Exec Paid for Beating," *Newsday*, July 28, 1955.
187. "Pleads Guilty to Attempted Forgery," *Sag Harbor Express*, January 15, 1959.
188. "3 Hoodlums Wreck Migrant Camp Hall," *Newsday*, September 5, 1957.
189. "Man Blinded by Attacker," *New York Times*, September 19, 1966.
190. *Mattituck Watchman*, May 2, 1974.
191. "Courts," *Long Island Traveler*, June 10, 1976.
192. "Town Police Nab Alleged Murderer of Farm Laborer," *Patchogue Advance*, October 9, 1947.
193. "Migrant Admits Fatal Stabbing," *Newsday*, October 10, 1955. Eddie G. House was a blues artist known as Son House whose early influences included artists Robert Johnson and Muddy Waters. By the 1940s, he was retired from music and living in Rochester, New York, before entering the migrant stream and finding work on Long Island. It is unclear how much time he spent in jail for the crime; however, a decade later, Son House was free to resume his musical career until his death in 1988.
194. "Say Gambling Losses Led to Camp Murder," *Newsday*, February 5, 1953.
195. "Migrant Sentenced for Fatal Stabbing," *Patchogue Advance*, April 16, 1959.
196. "Man Held in Killing," *Newsday*, August 11, 1966.
197. "Youthful Laborer Charged with Manslaughter," *Long Island Traveler Mattituck Watchman*, November 16, 1957.
198. "Pleaded Innocent," *Long Island Traveler*, September 26, 1974.
199. "One of Three Defendants Pleads Guilty in L. Ronkonkoma Holdup," *Patchogue Advance*, November 13 ,1947.
200. "Bullets Fly During Riot, 3 Shot, 1 Held," *Newsday*, August 18, 1952.
201. "Crew Leader Shot and Killed in Mattituck," *Long Island Traveler-Mattituck Watchman*, October 10, 1957.
202. "Migrant Kills Migrant; Held for Grand Jury," *Sag Harbor Express*, January 15, 1959.
203. "Laborer Shot While Walking on Route 27A," *Long Island Traveler-Mattituck Watchman*, December 7, 1967.
204. "4 Arrested for 'Target Practice,'" *Newsday*, July 20, 1970.
205. "Man Stabbed to Death in Riverside," *County Review*, April 4, 1946.

206. "Hunt Knife Assailant of Cutchogue Potato Farmers," *Newsday*, August 23, 1952.

207. "Hollis Warner Slain; Charge Son," *Newsday*, August 9, 1967.

208. "Warner Is Sentenced for 2 Slayings," *Newsday*, June 29, 1968.

209. "4 Migrants Die in L.I. Labor Camp Blaze," *Newsday*, October 9, 1961.

210. "Camp Where Four Died Warned on Stoves," *Newsday*, October 18, 1961.

211. "Dark Days at the Cutchogue Labor Camp," *Suffolk Times*, September 26, 2014.

212. "LI Migrant Laborer Dies after Heater Explodes in Shack," *Newsday*, November 25, 1961.

213. "5 Children Die in L.I. Slum Blaze," *Newsday*, January 28, 1963.

214. "Farm Workers' House Burns, 3 Die," *Newsday*, January 15, 1968.

215. "Migrant Workers: A Challenge to Our Social Conscience," *Suffolk County News*, May 18, 1956.

216. *Harvest of Shame*.

217. *Newsday*, September 18, 1963.

218. "Bus Crash Kills 6 Migrants," *Newsday*, June 21, 1964.

219. "9 Are Killed and 16 Injured in Jersey Bus-Train Collision," *New York Times*, July 24, 1968.

220. "Jamaican Seriously Injured in Fall from Farm Truck," *Long Islander*, September 12, 1946.

221. *Newsday*, January 8, 1954.

222. "5 Killed in Weekend Crashes on LI Roads," *Newsday*, February 15, 1954.

223. *Long Islander*, August 11, 1960.

224. "3 Vehicles Collide in Fog," *Newsday*, November 8, 1978.

Chapter 6

225. "Supers to Back Migrant Labor Camp Clean-Up," *Patchogue Advance*, July 3, 1952.

226. "Town May Bond Those Operating Migrant Camps," *Patchogue Advance*, February 12, 1953.

227. "Farm Labor Camps in Brookhaven Town Are Given Health OK," *Patchogue Advance*, September 8, 1949.

228. "Two Farm Owners Fined," *Suffolk Count News*, September 26, 1957.

229. "New Sanitary Rules for Migrant Labor Camps," *Long Island Traveler*, December 18, 1958.

230. "134 Migrant Labor Camps in Suffolk; Increase 5-fold," *Patchogue Advance*, May 21, 1959. In 1951, there were 29 registered labor camps in the county. By 1958, there were 134 camps. Thus while the number of inspections in 1958 doubled from 1951, the number of camps had quadrupled over the same time period. While this might appear to skew the data, suggesting enhanced enforcement, the passage of the new laws certainly ushered in a period of stricter scrutiny at labor camps throughout Suffolk County.

231. "Officials Inspect Migrant Labor Camps on North Fork," *Long Island Traveler*, August 3, 1967.

232. Records of inspections prior to 1971 were lost or discarded by the Suffolk County Department of Health.

233. "Farm Workers' House Burns, 3 Die," *Newsday*, January 15, 1968.

234. "Bridgehampton; Camp Operator Arrested," *East Hampton Star*, June 1, 1967.

235. *Long Island Traveler*, February 8, 1968.

236. "11 Health Violations Laid to Migrant Boss," *Newsday*, September 10, 1968.

237. "Cutchogue Camp for Migrants Is Ordered Vacated," *Newsday*, January 17, 1970.

238. "Suffolk Migrant Labor Report Cites 965 Violations in Camps," *New York Times*, July 14, 1971.

239. "The Land Where the Crew Chief Is Boss," *Newsday*, May 21, 1978.

240. "Charges Labor Camp Operators," *Long Island Traveler*, October 30, 1975.

241. *Long Island Traveler*, November 6, 1975.

242. "Farm Worker Contractor Guilty of Tax Evasion," *Newsday*, July 28, 1977.

243. "Labor Camp Operates Without Permission," *Long Island Traveler*, September 4, 1975.

244. Ibid.

245. "Threats Follow Migrant Raids," *East Hampton Star*, November 13, 1975.

246. "Enforcing the Laws on Migrant Labor," *Newsday*, January 27, 1977.

247. Information on the result of this legal action was not readily available.

248. "Justice Closes a Labor Camp," *Newsday*, March 20, 1982.

249. Dufresne and McDonnell, "Migrant Labor Camps," 279–304.

250. "DA Admits Aide Usurped Judge's Power, Ran Trial," *Newsday*, April 19, 1955.

251. "Because DA Played Judge, Mechanic Wins Second Trial," *Newsday*, April 29, 1955.

252. "BH Pickle Grower Pays $250 Fine for Assault Conviction," *Southampton Press*, December 5, 1968.

253. "Stein, After Visit to L.I. Farms, Will Ask Laws to Aid Migrants," *New York Times*, September 16, 1971.

254. Oral interview by author with Karl Grossman, February 8, 2020. Mr. Grossman is an author and investigative journalist. He currently serves as a professor of journalism at the State University of New York/College at Old Westbury.

255. "Suffolk Chosen for Test Cases," *Newsday*, May 26, 1971.

256. "Judge Orders Free Access to Migrant Labor Camps," *New York Times*, October 4, 1971. See also Folgueras v. Hassle, 331, F. Supp 615 (W.D. Mich, 1971).

257. "They Give a Home to Migrants' Children," *Newsday*, August 22, 1958.

258. Tomkins and Tomkins, *Other Hampton*.

259. *Sag Harbor Express*, April 29, 1954.

260. *East Hampton Star*, September 10, 1959, and September 1, 1960.

261. Ibid., August 21, 1975.

262. "Churches to Help Migrant Workers," *Newsday*, September 24, 1949.

263. "Migrant Worker Problem Traced to Poor Camps," *Patchogue Advance*, September 18, 1952.

264. *Long Island Traveler*, November 29, 1956.

265. "Mobile Church Is Dedicated," *Patchogue Advance*, October 2, 1947.

266. "Helen Gray Smith Wins Kiwanis Club 'Man of the Year' Award," *Long Islander*, January 12, 1956.

267. Antionette Bosco, "The Migrant Labor Problem," April 17, 1969.

268. 1969 hearings, 22, 38.

269. "LI Migrants: Unresolved Plight," *Newsday*, June 23, 1972.

270. "Suffolk Panel Asks Migrant System's End," *Newsday*, November 21, 1967.

271. "Farmers Blast Migrant Phase-Out Bid," *Newsday*, November 22, 1967.

272. "A Vanishing Breed, Time Changes the Migrants' Lot," *Sunday News*, May 25, 1969.

273. 1969 hearings, 22, 38.

274. "Land Where Crew Chief."

275. "L.I. Volunteers Reports on Anti-Poverty Programs," *Long Island Advance*, June 9, 1966.

276. "A Boss Admits He Cheated Migrants," *Newsday*, June 27, 1972.

277. "Boxers Are Learning the Ropes," *Newsday*, May 8, 1970.

278. "Human Relations Unit to Hear Vols Chief," *Long Island Advance*, September 29, 1966; "Community Action Committee Offers Tutoring Classes," *Long Island Advance*, March 24, 1966.

279. "History of VISTA in Southold Is Recounted," *Long Island Traveler*, September 21, 1967.

280. "VISTA Brightens L.I. Migrant Camp," *New York Times*, December 23, 1965.

281. "Community Action Begins for Economic Assistance," *Long Island Traveler*, July 8, 1965; "Push Bid for Migrant Housing," *Newsday*, March 26, 1966.

282. "Migrants Get Help but Not Enough," *Newsday*, September 27, 1966.

283. The monthly dues amount of sixty-two cents has remained the same since 1972 and was derived from the average hourly pay rate that migrant workers received at the time.

284. "Rock Concert to Benefit E.F.W.A.," *Northport Journal*, April 11, 1975.

285. "L.I. Farm Workers, Backed by Union, Fighting Eviction," *New York Times*, December 19, 1972.

286. "Arthur Josh Herron, 87, Fought for Laborers' Rights," *Newsday*, February 9, 1998.

287. "Duck Processing Plant Signs with Union," *Long Island Traveler*, June 16, 1955.

288. "A&P Migrant Employees Win Medical Coverage," *Newsday*, January 9, 1974.

289. "Suffolk's Secret Problem," *Suffolk County News*, May 18, 1956–June 15, 1956.

290. Ibid., May 18, 1956.

291. "Suffolk's Secret Problem," *Suffolk County News*, May 18, 1956–June 15, 1956.

292. Oral interview by author with Joseph Grattan, February 21, 2020.

293. "Officers Hurt Answering Call," *Long Island Traveler-Watchmen*, October 16, 1975.

294. Oral interview by author with Leslie Mashmann, August 6, 2020.

295. "Suffolk Airs Issue of Farm Migrants," *New York Times*, July 11, 1953.

296. "Says State Agencies Neglecting Migrants," *Newsday*, August 18, 1958.

297. "U.S., State Probing LI Migrant Labor Abuses," *Newsday*, May 22, 1961.

298. "The Land Where Crew Chief Is Boss," *Newsday*, May 21, 1978.

299. "Suffolk's First Executive H. Lee Dennison Dies," *Newsday*, May 8, 1983.

300. Oral interview by author with Lee Koppelman, January 23, 2020.

301. "Migrant System Is Called Costly," *New York Times*, February 11, 1968.

302. *Northport Journal*, July 30, 1970.

303. Mr. Koppelman recalled a time when the county was a large producer of red potatoes, which contain a high sugar content and were particularly favored by the Cubans. However, the implementation of the United States' embargo against Cuba prevented all exports to that island, which hurt the

farmers in the area. "In protest to the embargo" stated Koppelman, "the farmers dumped large amounts of red potatoes into the Long Island Sound."
304. "LI Migrants: Unresolved Plight," *Newsday*, June 23, 1972.

Chapter 7

305. Southold is approximately eighteen miles east of Riverhead.
306. Van Scoy, *Big Duck and Eastern Long Island's*.
307. *Sag Harbor Express*, December 27, 1929.
308. "Duck Farm: There's No Place Left to Go," *Newsday*, July 23, 1964.
309. "L.I. Shows Experts Where U.S. Gets Poultry," *Newsday*, June 9, 1948.
310. "Long Island Duck Processing Cooperative Thrives," *New York Times*, December 17, 1957.
311. "Experts Blame Duck Farms for Decline of GSB Oysters," *Patchogue Advance*, April 12, 1951.
312. *Southampton Press*, October 6, 1960, and January 19, 1961.
313. "Phenomenal Growth of Oysters in South Bay," *Suffolk County News*, October 7, 1955.
314. "Duck Farms Polluted Bay," *Newsday*, July 17, 1956.
315. "2 Duck Farmers Polluting Bays, State Declares," *Suffolk County News*, June 5, 1958.
316. "Accuse Owners of Duck Farms," *Long Islander*, November 7, 1963.
317. "RFK Warns on Water Pollution," *Long Island Advance*, September 22, 1966.
318. "Duck Farms Cleanup Ordered," *Newsday*, July 29, 1972.
319. Long Island Duck Farm and Ecosystem Restoration Opportunities Report.
320. Ibid.
321. Hoffman, "Migrant Workers Lived."
322. *Long Island Advance*, July 2, 1964.
323. "Gifts Flow into Slum; CORE Head Stays Out," *Newsday*, July 27, 1964.
324. Many migrant workers settled in various parts of Suffolk County, including the Church Lane area of Cutchogue, New York. The end of World War I brought a period known as the Great Migration, when many Black farmworkers settled in other parts of Suffolk County, including the Church Lane community in Cutchogue. McGovern and Bernstein, "Preserving Church Lane."
325. "LI Migrants: Unresolved Plight," *Newsday*, June 23, 1972.

326. "Squalor, Official Inaction Equal Death in Suffolk's Slums," *Newsday*, February 11, 1959.

327. *Newsday*, September 24, 1964.

328. "Road Map to Squalor; LI Slums," *Newsday*, February 1, 1963.

329. "U.S., State Probing LI Migrant Labor Abuses," *Newsday*, May 22, 1961.

330. "Machines Take Jobs, Driving Migrants to Rural Slums," *New York Times*, September 2, 1960.

331. "Road Map to Squalor; LI Slums," *Newsday*, February 1, 1963.

332. Ibid.

333. "Will Suffolk County be Slumlord?" *Newsday*, February 16, 1963; "Riverhead Slum Drive Dies; Board Cites Cost," *Newsday*, March 2, 1960.

334. "Riverhead Asks State to Act on Slums," *Newsday*, April 8, 1959.

335. "U.S. Aide Call LI Slum Among Worst," *Newsday*, July 21, 1964.

336. "Long Island's Migrants," *Newsday*, September 1, 1961.

337. "Fear Project May Be Ghetto in Riverhead," *Newsday*, December 10, 1965.

338. "Suffolk Helps Ex-Farm Workers to Build Their Own Homes," *New York Times*, May 4, 1969.

339. "Riverhead OK's Code," *Newsday*, July 31, 1968.

340. "Slum Area Included in $4 Million Suffolk Wetlands Program," *Newsday*, November 15, 1962.

341. "Suffolk Exec Says Slum Homes Razed," *Newsday*, July 29, 1963.

342. "Action Against Sub-Standard Housing Taken," *Long Island Advance*, July 11, 1963.

343. "Relocation of Slum Families Aided by Firm," *Long Island Advance*, August 6, 1964.

344. "Riverhead Slum Shanties Are Destroyed," *Long Island Advance*, December 31, 1964.

345. *Patchogue Advance*, November 6, 1952.

346. "3 Children Killed in Shanty Blaze," *Newsday*, January 30, 1959.

347. "The Sum of Squalor and Inaction: Death," *Newsday*, February 11, 1959.

348. "3 More Die in LI Slum Fires," *Newsday*, February 9, 1959.

349. "Riverhead Slum Fire Kills Man; Town Acts," *Newsday*, February 4, 1959.

350. "Slum Fire Kills Riverhead Man; 7th Victim of '59," *Newsday*, June 15, 1959.

351. "2 Babies Die in Fire," *Suffolk County News*, May 2, 1963.

352. "Cabbages and Kings," *Suffolk County News*, May 9, 1963.

353. "Spanish Magee's Trail of Tears," *Newsday*, February 27, 1982.

Chapter 8

354. "A Fruitful Harvest: 36 Years of Tending Suffolk's Farms," *Newsday*, December 16, 1971.

355. "Machines Take Jobs, Driving Migrants to Rural Slums," *New York Times*, September 2, 1960.

356. "Migrant Labor: Why It's so Often Indispensable," *New York Times*, March 28, 1982.

357. Garcia-Colon, *Colonial Migrants*, 167.

358. "The Hard Life of Migrant Alley," *Newsday*, June 7, 1998.

359. "The Changing Face of the Suffolk Harvest," *New York Times*, October 6, 2002.

360. "LI Potato Acreage Down," *Newsday*, August 15, 1975.

361. "The Last Potato Graders," *Newsday*, April 2, 2005.

362. "Suffolk Loses Title as State's Most Lucrative Agricultural Producer," *Newsday*, March 5, 2015. The Long Island Farm Bureau cited the increased demand for yogurt products as the reason the upstate counties, which are dairy based, were able to overtake Suffolk County as the top agricultural producer in the state.

363. In 1970, New York State placed a statewide ban on Dichlorodiphenyltrichloroethane, commonly known as DDT, and restricted the use of up to sixty other pesticides. Federal bans on these pesticides were already in place before this ban.

364. "Scientists Curbing Potato Beetle," *Long Island Traveler-Watchman*, June 5, 1975.

365. "Farms Continue Decline in State," *New York Times*, February 1, 1964.

366. "LI's Land Squeeze," *Newsday*, October 5, 1968.

367. The term *agritainment* refers to agricultural-based entertainment, where tourists make up a substantial part of the target market. Such strategies that are used include U-Pick or Pick-Your-Own products, petting zoos, hayrides, corn mazes and children's discovery farms.

368. "John Wickham, 85, Innovative Farmer in Suffolk County," *New York Times*, February 28, 1994. John Wickham's son Tom explained that his father derived the idea of growing fruit on Long Island during a trip he had made to Argentina to study the fruit growing process. While there, he realized that the climate in the higher elevations of that country were similar to the climate on Long Island. Oral interview by author with Tom Wickham, July 30, 2020.

369. "Suffolk Closeup: Toasting the Hargraves, Pioneers of Wine Country," *Shelter Island Reporter*, June 8, 2012.

370. New York State. "Farm Laborers."
371. Ibid.

Epilogue

372. Rev Arthur Cullen Bryant. Find a Grave.
373. 1969 hearings, 23, 39.
374. Ibid., 18, 34.
375. "Farewell for a Friend of the Migrants," *Newsday*, January 25, 1971.
376. Sidney Schaer and Jim Scovel, "Migrant Advocate to Leave," *Newsday*, December 1, 1970.
377. NPR, "Maria Hinojosa."
378. Prince, "My Migrant Labor Camp," 92.
379. *Suffolk Times*, October 6, 2015.
380. Obituaries, *Newsday*, November 23, 1977.
381. "Human Relations Unit to Hear Vols Chief," *Long Island Advance*, September 29, 1966; "Community Action Committee Offers Tutoring Classes," *Long Island Advance*, March 24, 1966.
382. "L.I. Volunteers Reports on Anti-Poverty Programs," *Long Island Advance*, June 9, 1966.
383. "Migrant Committee May Have Further Hearings," *Long Island Traveler*, September 22, 1966.
384. "Mary Chase Stone, 66, Friend of Riverhead Migrant Workers," *Newsday*, November 23, 1977.
385. "Hear Mary Chase Stone Speak," *East Hampton Star*, May 2, 1968.
386. "L.I. Volunteers Reports on Anti-Poverty Programs," *Long Island Advance*, June 9, 1966.
387. "Human Relations Unit."
388. "Watkins-Johnson, 99, Believed in the Power of Prayer," *Suffolk Times*, March 24, 2020.
389. Obituary of Alan F. Perl, *New York Times*, December 12, 2002.
390. Hunter College, "Alan Perl."
391. "Morton Silverstein, Documentarian Who Explored Social Ills, Dies at 86," *New York Times*, October 12, 2016.
392. "A Man's Wish for His Mother in Discovering a Mother's Grave," *Newsday*, May 10, 2009.

BIBLIOGRAPHY

Aronson, Harvey. "Long Island's Migrants." *Newsday*, August 30, 1961.

Booth, Antonia. "Labor Camps in Migrant Alley: A Brief History." *Peconic Bay Shopper: Preserving Your North Fork History*, July 2, 2012.

Cashman, John. "Migrants Die in LI Labor Camp Blaze." *Newsday*, October 9, 1961.

County Review (Riverhead, New York).

Dufrense, Elizabeth J., and John J. McDonnell. "The Migrant Labor Camps: Enclaves of Isolation in our Midst." *Fordham Law Review* 40, no. 2 (1971): 279–304.

East Hampton (New York) *Star*.

Fleming, Geoffrey K., and Amy Kasuga Folk. *Munnawhatteaug: The Last Days of the Menhaden Industry on Eastern Long Island*. Southold, NY: Southold Historical Society, 2011.

Harvest of Shame. CBS Productions, 1960.

Holley, Michael. "Disadvantaged by Design: How the Law Inhibits Agricultural Guest Workers from Enforcing Their Rights." *Hofstra Law Review* 18, no. 2 (2001): 575–624.

Ismael Garcia-Colon. "Claiming Equality: Puerto Rican Farmworkers in Western New York." *Latino Studies*, 2008.

———. *Colonial Migrants at the Heart of Empire: Puerto Rican Workers on U.S. Farms*. Oakland: University of California Press, 2020.

Long Island Duck Farm and Ecosystem Restoration Opportunities Report, U.S. Army Corps of Engineers, New York District, and Suffolk County, February 2009.

Long Island Press (Syosset, NY).

Long Island Traveler (Cutchogue, NY).

Long Island Traveler, Mattituck Watchman (Southold, NY).

Long-Islander (Huntington, NY).

McGovern, Allison Manfra, and David J. Bernstein. "Preserving Church Lane: Applied Anthropology and History in a Long Island African-American Community." *Long Island History Journal* 23, no. 2 (2013). https://lihj.cc.stonybrook.edu.

Newsday.

New York State Interdepartmental Committee on Farm and Food Processing Labor. New York's Harvest Labor. Report Covering the 5-Year Period 1943–1948. Albany, 1949.

New York Times.

North Fork Life, July 1, 1943.

Northport Journal.

Patchogue (NY) *Advance.*

Payne, Les. "Waiting for the Eagle to Fly." *Newsday,* July 11, 1970.

Prince, Helen. "My Migrant Labor Camp School 1949–1961." *Long Island Forum* 52, no. 3 (August 1, 1989): 85–99.

Sag Harbor (New York) *Express.*

Scoy, Susan Van. *The Big Duck and Eastern Long Island's Duck Farming Industry.* Charleston, SC: Arcadia Publishing, 2019.

Shelter Island Reporter.

Sherman, Lawrence J., and Joan L. Levy, "Free Access to Migrant Labor Camps," *American Bar Association Journal* 57, no. 5 (May 1971): 434–37.

Southampton Press.

Squire, Paul. "Dark Days at the Cutchogue Camp." *Suffolk Times,* September 26, 2014.

Suffolk County News (Sayville, NY).

Tomkins, Calvin, and Judy Tomkins. *The Other Hampton.* New York: Grossman Publishers, 1974.

U.S. Department of Agriculture. *Wage and Wage Rates of Potato Harvest Workers on Long Island, New York, Week Ended September 1, 1945.* Washington, D.C., March 1946.

What Harvest for the Reaper? January 29, 1968, in NET Journal. Produced by National Educational Television and Radio Center. Thirteen WNET,

Library of Congress, American Archive of Public Broadcasting. https://americanarchive.org.

Wick, Steve. *Heaven and Earth: The Last Farmers of the North Fork*. New York: St. Martin's Press, 1996.

Wilcox, Leroy. "Duck Industry." In *Long Island: A History of Two Great Counties, Nassau and Suffolk*. Vol. 2, by Paul Bailey, 440–58. New York: Lewis Historical Publishing, 1949.

Websites

Bracero History Archive. Center for History and New Media. http://braceroarchive.org.

Britannica. "Long Island." https://www.britannica.com.

Find a Grave. Rev Arthur Cullen Bryant. https://www.findagrave.com.

Hoffman, David. "The Migrant Workers Lived in Duck Houses." August 21, 2009. https://www.youtube.com.

Hunter College. "Alan Perl." Center for Puerto Rican Studies. https://centropr.hunter.cuny.edu.

Jaicks, Nancy Robin. "Race, Ethnicity and Class on Shelter Isand, 1652–2013." Long Island History Journal. https://lihj.cc.stonybrook.edu.

Lariccia, Ben, and Joe Tucciarone. "Bound for America: The Padrone System of Contract Labor (Part 1)." La Gazzetta Italiana. April 2019. https://www.lagazzettaitaliana.com.

National Labor Relations Board. https://www.nlrb.gov.

New York Department of State Division of Corporations. https://appext20.dos.ny.gov.

New York State. "Farm Laborers Fair Labor Practices Act." Department of Labor. https://www.labor.ny.gov.

NPR. "Maria Hinojosa." https://www.npr.org.

Reilly, Jacklyn. "Agricultural Laborers: Their Inability to Unionize Under the National Labor Relations Act." Penn State Law. https://pennstatelaw.psu.edu/_file/aglaw/Publications_Library/Agricultural_Laborers.pdf.

Rivera, Geraldo. "Migrants Dirt Cheap." *Eyewitness News*. July 26, 1972. https://kaltura.uga.edu/media/t/1_6sipd92x/33785631.

Sylvester Manor Educational Farm. https://www.sylvestermanor.org.

ABOUT THE AUTHOR

Mark A. Torres is a husband, father, attorney and author.

Mark is the author of two fictional crime novels titled *A Stirring in the North Fork* (2015) and *Adeline* (2019), both available on Amazon, and a labor union–related children's book titled *Good Guy Jake* (Hard Ball Press, 2017).

Mark is also a labor and employment attorney who tirelessly represents thousands of unionized workers and their families throughout the greater New York area. Mark has a law degree from Fordham University School of Law and a bachelor's degree in history from New York University. Mark achieved his academic milestones while working full time as a refrigeration engineer at New York University and attending class in the evenings, all while raising a family. Mark's commitment to the labor movement spans longer than thirty years.